This is Our Village
Fulbourn

Published 2011 by arima publishing
www.arimapublishing.com

ISBN 978 1 84549 494 0

Printed and bound in the United Kingdom
Typeset in Calibri, 12pt

Swirl is an imprint of arima publishing.
arima publishing
ASK House, Northgate Avenue
Bury St Edmunds, Suffolk IP32 6BB
t: (+44) 01284 700321, www.arimapublishing.com

Acknowledgements

We would like to offer our gratitude to the many individuals and organisations, without whose support we wouldn't have been able to produce this anthology.

Fulbourn Arts, for their initial funding and support.

The various contributors and speakers at our monthly meetings, who inspired much of the writing here – Terry Dash from Meldreth History Society for starting us off; Michael Beaumont, John White and Richard Wombwell, for their tales of growing up in the village and the changing shops; Andrew Tanser, for sharing his vision of the Fulbourn Wall; Midge Gillies, for her talk on writing and researching; Edye Hoffman, for unfailingly making the coffee.

Fiona Thorpe, Head Teacher of Fulbourn Primary School, for her co-operation.

The Co-operative Community Fund, for providing the funds allowing us to publish.

Pat White and many others of the Fulbourn Village History Society, for providing us with access to their great range of records and photographs.

Richard Franklin of arima Publishing, for his expert help and encouragement.

FULBOURN
VILLAGE LIBRARY

Contents

Part 3: Hopes and fears for the future

Foreword

With archaeological remains dating back to the Neolithic period, the site of Fulbourn has long been recognized as a good one for human habitation. The Roman Road from Colchester to Cambridge passes just 1 mile away; Fleam Dyke, an Anglo-Saxon fortification, ends in the village; there were three manors here in the Middle Ages and two churches from around 1100 to 1776; a population of 2,500 by the beginning of the twentieth century, grown to 5,000 by the year 2000. But the advantages of earlier times can become the threats of today. With a slim Green Belt separating the village from Cambridge, with ever-growing pressure for more housing, can the village survive as a thriving sustainable community through this millennium and into the next?

At present most of the resources needed to support that community lie within the village itself. However, a Tesco Superstore just half a mile away threatens the High Street shops, and no replacement premises have been found for our Post Office, which closed when the last owners retired in October 2010. Infilling, and the re-generation of the large Windmill housing Estate which was built in the 60s, is producing a more intensively built environment. So far, 88 properties have been (or are about to be) demolished, and they are (or will be) replaced by 178 properties of varied size.

The Writing Group

The Housing Association involved in this re-generation, Accent Nene, has inadvertently been the spur to this Writing Group. They have replaced an old community centre with our brand new Library and Meeting room, in conjunction with the Parish Council. They also appointed an artist, Andrew Tanser, to develop some community sculpture, and one of his ideas was a village Life Wall. This will depict various images from the past on one side, and from the present on the other. What about the future? We thought we might tackle past, present and future through writing about what the Village means to us, how it has already coped with changes over the years, what we hope for in the future.

When we began we were just some twenty residents of Fulbourn, not sure whether we had been coerced into joining a group, worried about making fools of ourselves, and wondering whether we were capable of writing anything anyone would be interested in. Six months later we have overcome our fears, and put into words the interest, passion and commitment to our community and our village, that made us join in the first place.

We've been joined by Year 6 of the Village Primary School, who really took the future to heart, and their poems give us much.

We hope you enjoy reading the results.

Gill Aslett and Helen Kingsley
Writing Group Co-ordinators

Rowan class

Always eager to encourage children to write I was delighted when Fulbourn Primary School's Year 6 class (Rowan) was invited to take part in this project. Our learning for the Spring term was largely focused on the environment and sustainability which dovetailed perfectly with thinking about Fulbourn 2050. So, where did we begin?

Many of our pupils are, thankfully, very aware of environmental issues so when I asked them to imagine what the village of Fulbourn might be like in the future they were full of ideas. Interestingly, the children quickly and naturally divided into two schools of thought: those who imagined a bleak future and those who took a much more positive stance, believing that everyone will rally to ensure the village thrives.

Learning about any literary genre at Fulbourn Primary always begins with reading what others have written. We read poems by famous poets and unknown, poems around themes, funny poems and sombre poems, poems that rhyme and those that don't, poems written recently and poems written a century ago, poems to make you ponder and poems that don't even appear to be poems! Rowan class's enthusiasm for and interest in poetry began to stir!

We learned about literary devices - personification, rhythm and rhyme, metaphor and simile, repetition - their effect and impact on the reader. We brainstormed some of the issues around sustainability and the environment, discussing why these issues were significant and recording pertinent words and phrases. Reflecting on how they feel about living in Fulbourn the children spoke proudly of their village and its amenities. These personal responses formed the basis for finding and establishing their voice.

The poems which you find here are the children's own work. As part of the writing process, and with guidance, they have drafted, altered, improved and edited. We hope you enjoy reading the poems and catching a glimpse of the creativity and attitudes of Rowan class, 2010-2011.

Claire Creamer
Year 6 teacher and Literacy Leader.
Fulbourn Primary School.

Rooted
In
The
Past

Fulbourn Village Library – Past and Present

How to run a volunteer library?

First, find some premises,
Second, find some volunteers,
Third, find some books.

If only it were that simple.......

For me it all began in March 2003 with an innocent looking flyer landing on the doormat, asking if I could spare a couple of hours a month to help in the Library. I wasn't even a Library member but, as a relative newcomer to the village, I saw it as a good way to become involved in the community.

What I didn't fully appreciate was that the flyer was the unhappy result of several years of campaigning and fundraising by The Friends of Fulbourn Library, a group that was set up in 1995 when 20 libraries were identified for possible closure. Fortunately Fulbourn Library was saved that year but the threat never really went away, so The Friends continued their activities. According to records, there had been a Library in Fulbourn since 1878 so to remove this facility after all these years was inconceivable to many.

However, early in 2003, The Friends lost their battle; Fulbourn was amongst 10 libraries to be closed by the County Council. The villages were offered a weekly visit from a mobile library, but in response to protests, the County Council challenged residents to come up with a business plan for a library. Naturally The Friends rose to this challenge and together with the Parish Council and Fulbourn Primary School Governors they formed a consortium which drew up a 3-year business plan, and after a lot of hard work the first Service Level Agreement with the County Council to run our volunteer Library, named a 'Library Access Point' by the Library Service, was signed.

Those who had responded to the aforementioned flyer were invited to attend a meeting in June 2003 and the beginnings of a volunteer run library emerged. I must add at this point that there were no librarians amongst us. Prior to opening, each volunteer had to be CRB checked and 12 of us attended a one-day training course on the County Council's Library Management System, 'Cambook'. The County Council gave us £3,000 as a start-up grant, one computer for book issues, 2 computers for public use (all with broadband connection) plus 1,000 brand new books, with the promise to rotate these books throughout the year with another Library Access Point. They also left us with the books in the Local Studies and Reference sections. The County Council run Library closed in October and we re-opened it on Saturday 22 November 2003, following many hours of organising the shelves, sorting through all of the donated books and sticking date labels and bar codes into them. A member of the County Library Service came to talk to us one afternoon to guide us on our way and gave 3 of us about 15 minutes training on how to accept the County books into our Library and how to catalogue our donated books. Luckily she left us a set of instructions!

And so we began our exciting new venture: operating from the same premises, The Old School Building in School Lane, continuing the same opening hours, 13½ hours per week over 7 sessions every day except Sunday, but sharing the room with a class from the Primary School.

We got off to a slow start during the winter months, learning as we went along, but as our stock grew with the constant stream of donated books and word got round that we had better books than the Library Service had been providing in recent years, our visitor and borrowing figures gradually increased. We spread the word by leafleting every household in Fulbourn and advertising in neighbouring villages and in 'The Mill'.

As we hadn't had a 'grand opening' we decided to celebrate our 1st birthday by holding a social event with a variety of guest speakers and entertainers. We also had a private celebration in The Six Bells for volunteers plus partners which has become an annual event as it is such a good opportunity for us all to get together. It's amazing how much noise a group of 'librarians' can make!

After sharing our space with the School for 18 months we were really excited in March 2005 when the School group moved upstairs in the building, enabling us to occupy the whole of the Library space. We were able to purchase more shelves to accommodate our growing number of books and to provide a few comfortable chairs for reading and relaxation.

However, early in 2006 the situation didn't look quite so rosy. Although the School was meant to be managing the Old School Building, negotiations were still taking place over its transfer from the County Council to the School. The County Council was also threatening to close more libraries, and possibly Library Access Points, if the Council Tax rise was not high enough. Fortunately for the Library, although not so good for Council Tax payers, the rise was sufficient to avoid any closures and we then received news that the County Council was willing to renew our Service Level Agreement for a further 3 years, subject to an acceptable business plan.

Life in the Library continued as normal and in July 2006 we were faced with another big challenge; the introduction of a new Library Management System, 'Unicorn'. Eleven of us went to Cambridge Central Library for 3 hours training; then we were let loose on our public, once again with a set of instructions. We are very fortunate in Fulbourn to have such understanding customers who supported us then with the anomalies of a new computer system and continue to do so when we don't do something quite right.

As we were about to sign our new 3-year Agreement with the County Council, 2006-2009, we received the news that the School wanted to hand back the management of The Old School Building to the County Council as the running costs were too high. We did, however, have a little breathing space as the School was persuaded to continue until September 2007, so the Agreement was signed and numerous meetings followed regarding the future of the Library. It seemed the

County Council had no further use for the Old School Building and was concerned about the condition of the central heating boiler and the general state of the roof and brickwork.

Just when we were beginning to think things couldn't get much worse, there was a fire at the Library one Sunday afternoon in April 2007. It began in an outhouse and fortunately the alarm was raised very promptly preventing it spreading into the Library. The roof of our storeroom was affected and the smoke damage was quite extensive. But with a lot of hard work and cleaning, we were open for business as usual by 3pm the following day. The smell, however, lingered for months!

The regeneration of the Windmill Estate provided us with the only realistic option for re-housing the Library and we were so lucky that the timing was just right. By the end of 2007, thanks to the Parish Council and Accent Nene, a new home had been secured in the community building to be built in the first phase of the redevelopment, now known as The Swifts. Our visitor numbers and books issues increased during this year due to the temporary closure of Cambridge Central Library and due to our higher profile in village news.

Apart from continuing to run the Library in an eerily empty Old School Building, where the County Council agreed we could remain until the end of 2008, that year was spent discussing the design of the new building and Library, and securing funds for the new shelving and furniture. None of which went particularly smoothly. Unfortunately the County Council seemed reluctant to allow us to stay longer, but following intervention by the Library Service and our County Councillor, the County Council was persuaded that the building wasn't about to fall down in the next few months. We celebrated by having a birthday party for our Library in the Old School Building – its 5th!

Old Library, School Lane

New Library, Haggis Gap

In May 2009 our long-awaited move to The Swifts became a reality. We were only closed for 2 days – one to pack and one to un-pack. Our volunteers really excelled themselves and we had a huge amount of fun. Reaction to our new premises was really positive, making all our hard work worthwhile, and we adapted really quickly to our new environment. Later that year another business plan was produced and an Agreement was signed with the County Council for 2009-2012.

Rather naively, we hoped that all our challenges were behind us, but in 2010 the threat of County Council cuts faced us once again and it seemed there was little room for negotiation this time. Fortunately the value of volunteer-run community libraries was recognised by the politicians, so we live to fight another day with reduced level of service from the County Council.

We have accepted these unavoidable cuts with grace as experience has taught us to continue running the Library whatever is going on around us. Since we began we have had a dedicated and enthusiastic volunteer force of over 40 people, sadly some move on and some pass on, but new people continue to join. Many of us have been involved since the very beginning. We aren't professionals but we try our best to provide as professional a service as we can. Each year we promote the National Reading Challenge, which runs over the school holidays and is enjoyed by all the children participating. Over the years we have held many events; author events, family history evenings, poetry and writing events, either independently or as part of Fulbourn Arts Festival, and we have produced an anthology to celebrate the life of Charles Darwin. We are really fortunate to have the support of the community who continue to borrow books from us and continue to donate books to us and with their support we hope to continue for many years to come.

Kathy Attmore

St Vigor's church clock and the clock winder

FOREWORD

When I decided to research some of the history of St Vigor's Church clock and the role of the *Clock Winder* I found myself swept up in a story that goes back 800 years. It was during the reigns of Richard the Lion Heart and King John that clocks which chimed the hour first made their appearance in England.

To me history is a gloriously alive subject confirmed by the fact that the clock in St Vigor's Church installed in 1775 still performs its function of an hourly chime - in recent years thanks to the tireless dedication of Horace White, the present landlord of the Six Bells Pub, backed up by his son Hugo and brother John.

BACKGROUND

A Turret Clock[1] is a public clock on the outside of a building with a dial linked to a bell which chimes on the hour, or part of an hour. Early clocks had astronomical features showing the sun, moon and stars. The earliest primitive clocks probably evolved in monasteries. In Chris McKay's book (Church Clocks) he found a record of a fire at St. Edmundsbury Abbey (Bury St Edmunds) in 1198 where the monks used some water from their clock to put out the fire! This is evidence of a very early Water Clock.

It is believed that monks hung a small primitive clock on a wall with an alarm, which resulted in a monk ringing a bell to bring the community together. This naturally developed into a clock, which triggered the automatic ringing of a bell.

---

[1] Some horological experts prefer the term Tower Clock or Church Clock.

Over time clocks spread to more and more monasteries, convents, churches and palaces. The advent of great country houses led to each estate having a Turret Clock to summon the workers; followed by barracks, town halls, railway stations and of course the world's most famous clock chime of Big Ben. The sound of the Westminster chime has a deep resonance in the British psyche with its association with the evening BBC News and the *Mother of Parliaments*.

ST VIGOR'S CHURCH

St Vigor's Church is more than 900 years old and was almost certainly built by one of William the Conqueror's noblemen after 1066. The name of St Vigor's is very rare amongst English churches but Vigor was a well-established Norman saint who had been a missionary in Northern France and became the Bishop of Bayeux in the sixth century.

It is strange to relate that at one time there were two Norman churches in the middle of Fulbourn almost side by side, All Saints and St Vigor's. At the back of St Vigor's Church are recorded the names of the clergymen from both churches commencing with the first Rector of St Vigor's, John de Sweinstorp in 1198 and the first Vicar of All Saints, Robert de Pelham in 1234.

All Saints Church was fatally wrecked in a massive storm on May 31st 1766 when the tower and five bells collapsed leaving a scene of terrible devastation resulting in the decision to demolish the church.

In order to carry out the plan and use St. Vigor's for both congregations it was necessary to apply for an Act of Parliament, which would stipulate the terms and conditions of such a merger including the financial ramifications and the long term employment of both clergymen. The name of the church then became St Vigor's and All Saints and there continued to be two clergymen until 1876.

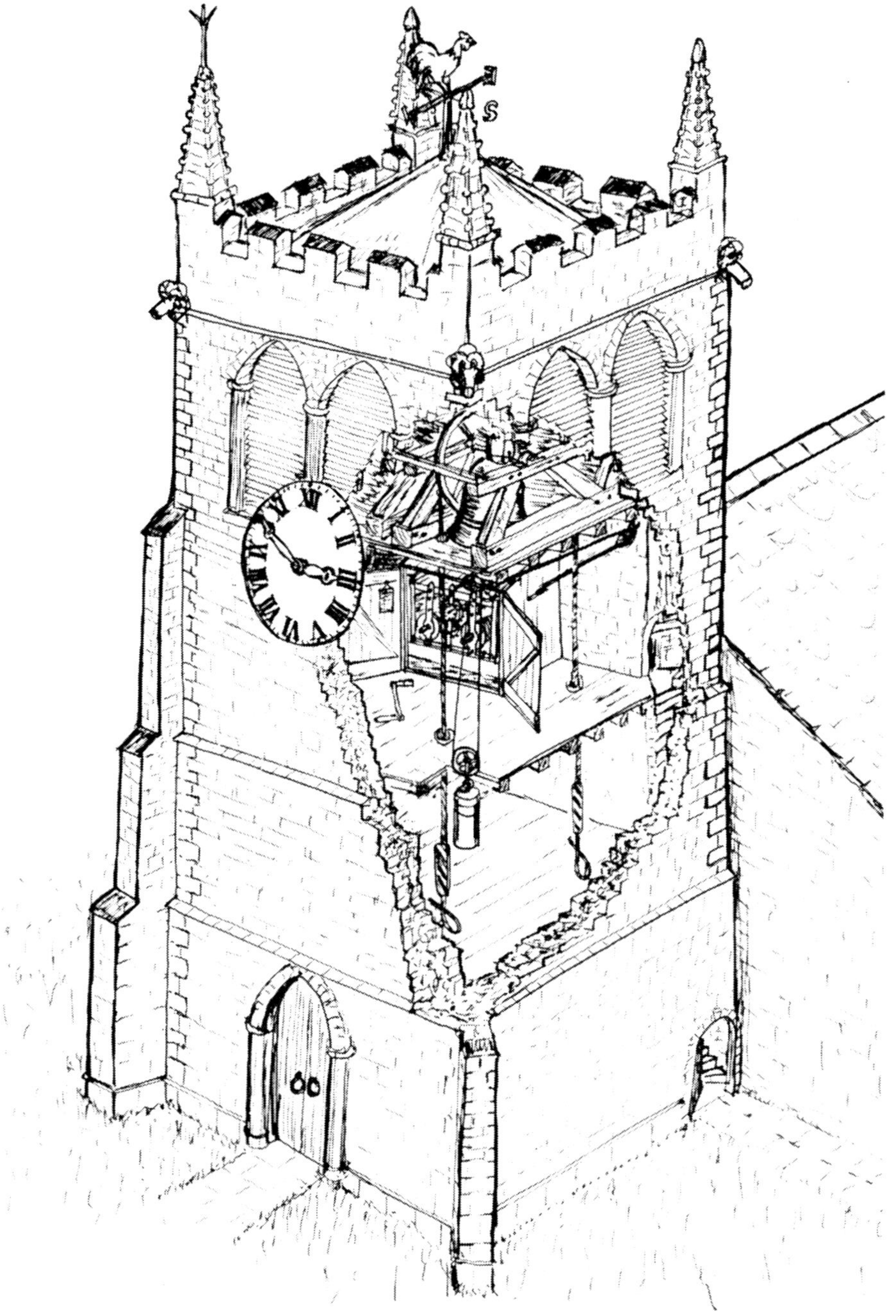

Sectioned drawing of a Church Clock by John Ablott

KEEPING TIME

Today our notion of time is very different from the experience of our ancestors. We wear a wristwatch and carry a mobile phone with a 24-hour clock and a laptop with the time and date. Life is fast and confined by a series of deadlines. A typical working day has a set pattern; rising at a certain time, leaving the house to a catch a train and clocking in and out of work. We watch 24-hour news and sporting events timed to a split second. Television and radio demand programme times.

Immediate access to accurate time is very recent. For most of our existence people have worked on the land, rising at dawn, working in the fields all day and returning home at dusk. The season, weather and the amount of sunlight controlled all daily activities except for the sound of a church bell on Sunday mornings calling parishioners to church.

In the Middle Ages time was measured with a sundial, which gives different lengths of time in winter and summer. The more sophisticated division of the day only existed in churches, monasteries and convents for services and mealtimes. For over a thousand years, time was measured by sundials or water clocks, marked candles, or hourglasses. The most accurate method was a water clock, which fed water between two containers at a precise rate.

The feudal system of serfs working on their master's land during set seasons did not require a precise measurement of time. It was not until an hourly wage became normal that both master/employer and worker demanded more accurate measurement of an hour. A key period in England was the impact of the plague in 1384, which produced a huge shortage of labour and a rare flexing of bargaining power by the surviving workers. An hourly rate of pay for different trades was slowly introduced.

When clocks were designed to strike the hour the sound of the chime was more important than a dial that told the hour. All the early clock faces on church towers were either blank or had astronomical signs of the sun, moon and stars. The first mechanical clocks built in England appear between 1280 and 1300. Examples include:

Dunstable Priory 1283
Old St Paul's 1286
Merton College 1288
Norwich Priory 1290
Ely Abbey 1291
Canterbury Cathedral 1291

The ecclesiastical day was not divided into hours but larger divisions of three to four hours: Matins, Prime, Tierce, Sext, None, Vespers and Compline.

The prize for the oldest surviving mechanical clock goes to Salisbury Cathedral with a date of at least 1386 but probably earlier. The early clockmakers were German and French but English blacksmiths and engineers mastered the trade and began to experiment themselves. Three hundred years later the first Clockmakers Guild was formed in 1631 and London became the world centre of clock making.

ST VIGOR'S CHURCH CLOCK

The first mention of St Vigor's Church Clock is 1525 during the reign of Henry VIII. However because the clock bell at the top of the church tower may date from the fifteenth century there remains the tantalizing possibility that St Vigor's could have had an even earlier clock.

Additional support for this possibility is the coincidence that the first Rector of St Vigor's took office in 1198, the same year as the fire at the Abbey in Bury St. Edmunds and the evidence of a water clock. These were two Norman institutions and it is almost certain that the Rector and Abbot were ecclesiastical colleagues sharing the technology of the time. It does not take much imagination to see how an early mechanical clock in the Abbey would have been noted in St Vigor's.

Fulbourn History Society and a record concerning Wright's Clock Land have revealed evidence for the 1525 clock.

'On the 16th April 1525 Robert Wright and Robert Casbred by deed poll enefoffed (granted possession) to Nicholas Wood and others of their heirs, 13 acres of land and another grant in that year to the same person, of another 10 acres. The profits from these lands were to be used to repair and keep in good order ***the clock in the Parish of St Vigor's*** *and towards ringing the curfew bell and the day bell from Michaelmas (September 29th) until St Mark's Day (April 25th). And any money left over should be used for the repair of the steeple and the bell.'*

The present clock is dated 1775 with the clockmaker, Thomas Safford, engraved on the mechanism. A second name of Theopolus Spendelow is added in 1805. To put these dates into historical context the first clock coincides with the outbreak of the American War of Independence and the second with the Battle of Trafalgar. The clock was last restored in 1935, by E C Sebley.

Thomas Safford was clearly a very well respected clock maker and repairer because in 1817 he overhauled a clock from Kings College, Cambridge made in 1671, which he removed and installed in St Giles Church, Cambridge where it remained until 1925 when it finally stopped working properly. It was removed and on the recommendation of the Director of Cambridge University Museum of Archaeology, it was donated to the Science Museum in London.

The second clock maker's name is Theopilus Spendelow. What a name and surely one that would have found favour with Charles Dickens in one of his novels! Sadly I have only been able to trace one reference in an obituary for a person with an identical name, a watchmaker who died in Cambridge on, or around December 7th 1781. This strongly suggests that this was the father of his identically named son. I have no information on Mr Sebley's work in 1935.

A typical feature of the present clock dial is that it was installed hundreds of years after the construction of the church tower. It is located in an awkward position low down the tower window and from some vantage points it is obscured by the church entrance. A similar second dial is on the rear of the tower. This odd position accords with the view that dials are generally a much later addition than the clock itself and were installed in the eighteenth or nineteenth centuries.

OLD CHURCH CLOCKS

It was only when I began researching St Vigor's clock that I realised how unique these mechanical timepieces are. They represent the oldest fully functioning mechanical appliances, which still perform their original purpose. They are not in a museum and are not restarted for a one off viewing. Despite the clock mechanism being hidden from view, the clock face and accompanying hourly chime still perform their original purpose of publicly telling the time on a clock dial and an hourly bell.

Whereas every week a group of bell ringers meet to practice or play a peel of bells for weddings and special events, the clock needs more frequent attention by just one person. It is a solitary task without glamour or status and for this reason many hand-wound clocks have been replaced by electrical motors or completely new electric clocks.

'Unlike domestic clocks with their requirement to be ornamental, these machines were built without pretension of show. Their beauty lies in the honest functioning of their gears and the polished metal of their precision parts. Their workings are open to view, their large scale and relative simplicity give them a friendly, toy-like quality, and the elementary system of levers, wires and hammers for striking bells gives them an enjoyable theatricality' (Church Clocks by Hugh Rock).

A Turret Clock has an enormous number of parts with a baffling range of evocative sounding names. Here are just a few: Birdcage, Bob, Click, Dog Clutch, Double Three Legged Gravity, Foliot, Going Train, Great Wheel, Jack – Monkey on the Rope, Night Silencing, Plate and Spacer, Snail, Ting Tang, Tune, Barrel, Waiting Train and Winding Jack.

THE CHURCH CLOCK WINDER

The earliest record of a Clock Winder or Clock Keeper is at Norwich Cathedral. *'In 1322 a new clock was installed in Norwich, an expensive replacement for an earlier clock dated 1273. This had a large two metre astronomical dial with automata and bells. The cost of the installation included the full-time employment of two clock keepers for two years'.*

Six hundred and thirty six years later Horace White of Fulbourn became the Church Winder of St Vigor's Church clock. He was 15 when he was offered the post in 1958 by the Revd. Arnold Swallow in return for some extra pocket money. It followed the retirement of the previous incumbent; Mr Monk aged 80, who found the climb too steep for his arthritic legs.

The Revd. Swallow, wife and children moved into the village in 1957 and were quickly befriended by the White family and the children all became very good friends. This knowledge of Horace would have been an obvious reason for the new Rector to put his faith in a boy he knew well.

For an interim period another local man, Nobby Clark, took over whilst Horace learnt about the art of clock winding, assisted by his older brother, John and younger brother David.

John White had the advantage of being a bell ringer since the age of eleven and his frequent trips to the Bell Tower offered him the sight of Mr Monk at work. John passed on this first-hand knowledge to his younger brother Horace. Except for a couple of years when Horace was away from the village he has steadfastly maintained the task of winding up the clock for over fifty years.

On one occasion when David was deputising for his brother Horace he decided to wind up the clock late at night. As he approached the church he was met by a policeman who asked what he was doing out so late at night.

David responded that he was about to wind up the church clock to which the constable replied '*Pull the other one*!' So David invited the constable to follow him to St Vigor's where he proceeded to confirm his story and dumbfound the officer of the law.

Every 48 hours Horace cycles or walks to St Vigor's, climbs the 29 steps up the tower and winds up the clock and chime. As you ascend the steep stone steps you are hit by an ancient smell of damp mustiness and a feeling that you are following in the footsteps of countless anonymous Clock Winders. It's cool and silent and the clock chamber is probably the most unknown part of the church. Unlike the group activity of bell ringers, the job of a Clock Winder is a solitary task. The inaccessibility of the chamber prevents all but a few interested guests viewing a marvel of preserved working machinery from the time of George III.

The design of the clock means it has to be wound every forty-eight hours. Horace chooses to do it four times a week. In the cramped clock chamber he steps up onto a raised wooden platform to reach the beautiful brass clock. It measures four feet by four feet and contains nine separate wheels of different sizes. It takes nineteen full turns of a giant handle called the *winding crank* to wind up the clock and six turns for the chime. With each turn two separate heavy weights are pulled up from a hole in the floor. The *winding crank* is very heavy and resembles the old jack handle once used to start a motorcar engine.

The long pendulum is affected by changes in heat and cold when the metal expands or contracts. Very occasionally a force of nature stops the clock. During the winter of 2010 the combination of heavy snow and freezing conditions made it impossible for the hands to move until there was a thaw.

On another occasion a weed called *fat hen* grew on the ledge in front of the clock face and began to cover the face itself. It had to be painstakingly removed to free up the hands.

The invasion of jackdaws is a common problem. In Horace's early years as the Clock Winder he arrived at a local pub for the Publican to say that the church clock was chiming eleven and he had stopped serving. Horace replied that it was not eleven until the chime stopped. So he got his pint but the bell continued to chime non-stop! He dashed back to the church and discovered a twig was jammed in the clock. He removed the twig and the bell fell silent.

In 2011 the problem has returned and a new bird proof screen is needed on the outside of the tower.

THE FUTURE

Of the four ancient churches serviced by the Fulbourn Rector, only St Vigor's Church Clock survives in its original form with a Clock Winder.

The Church of England requires parishes to maintain and preserve their Turret Clocks but they cannot ensure there are men or women prepared to wind them. The maintenance and associated costs for St. Vigor's Clock continues to be met from the charity originally started in 1525.

Not only are church clocks incredibly old, they are also part of the fabric of our culture. I hope the Fulbourn community will maintain its proud tradition of supporting a Clock Winder to service the St Vigor's Church Clock for many years to come.

David Horace Dobson

ACKNOWLEDGEMENTS

Much of my information on clocks has been obtained from two sources: (1) The Antiquarian Society Turret Clock Group and their *Turret Clock Keeper's Handbook* by Chris McKay and (2*) Church Clocks* by Hugh Rock. I am also very grateful to John Ablott for allowing me to reproduce his drawing of a Church Tower (St. Anne's Church, Limehouse) with its sectional design.

My own humble research was greatly assisted by members of the Fulbourn History Society, Cambridgeshire County Archives and Cambridge Central Library.

During the time this work was undertaken I was reminded that one of my Great Uncles, George Birchall was a London watchmaker and suddenly the story became more personal. I spoke to the Clerk of the Worshipful Company of Clock Makers of which he was a member and was referred on to various specialist sources of information.

In conclusion my thanks to: Horace White, John White, Mrs Swallow, David Wright and Fulbourn History Society.

Fulbourn in the nineteenth century

I have been reading Don Crane's *Fulbourn Chronicles* (extracts from a Cambridge newspaper concerning Fulbourn) and trying to imagine what the village was like in the late eighteenth and early nineteenth century. It was very different from today - no paved roads, no street lighting, many houses with outside toilets, the smell of farmyards wherever one went, and a lot of poverty among farmworkers. Cambridge must have seemed a long way off to poor families who had no transport. You either had to walk to get there or to find the money to pay for a ride on one of the carts which went regularly to and fro to collect supplies.

On the positive side this was still a fen village, so the wetter conditions would have encouraged many more wildflowers to grow, and children were able to ramble (safely on the whole) over large areas, bathe in ponds and get into trouble for sliding down haystacks and playing hide-and-seek in the farmers' barns. Many of them didn't go to school, or only attended school part of the time, when they were not needed to help on the family smallholding.

Farming families were the mainstay of the village community. At the very beginning of the nineteenth century many families who had lived in Fulbourn for three or four hundred years were still farming their strips in the common fields. Some had swapped and amalgamated their strips or reclaimed wasteland to create their own smallholdings over the centuries. Many small farmers ran shops or other businesses as well to supplement their income.

The Fulbourn Enclosure Act led to great changes in the farming community. Holdings in the common field were amalgamated or exchanged so that each owner had his own 'enclosure' which had by law to be surrounded by a hedge or fence. Carrying this out was expensive, and many smallholders were forced to sell their holdings to more prosperous members of the community, especially after the price of wheat fell drastically at the end of the Napoleonic wars. Thus many smallholders either had to leave the village to find work, or to become landless labourers who were at the mercy of the vicissitudes of economic life.

In the 1790s the largest farmers in the village were Thomas Oslar and Thomas Hancock. Thomas Oslar senior died in 1786 and his eldest son also died in 1795 leaving a young son. Thomas Hancock died without a direct heir in l811, soon after he sponsored the building of the Independent Chapel (now the URC church) which became the focus of religious and social life for many Fulbourn families. These old yeoman families who had been connected with the village for centuries were soon replaced by new farming families who moved in from elsewhere to settle on the larger farms created by the Enclosure Act; but many of these newcomers married daughters of local farmers, so that although some names died out the bloodlines continued.

Thomas Hancock left his farmhouse and land to a cousin, John Chaplin, who came from the village of Clare. John Chaplin's sons became millers and maltsters as well as farmers and built up a substantial business. In about 1812 the Wright family moved into Hall Farm which they initially rented from the Townleys; another Wright family moved from Upwell into Rectory Farm in about 1850. The Paynes, who had come to the village in the 1790s and married into the Manning family, also farmed substantial holdings; considerable acres owned by Cambridge Colleges were let out to tenants like the Wells family who were at Queen's farm from about 1797 to 1865. In the 1870s farming again hit the doldrums and several farmers sold up. Towards the end of the century the Whites and Laceys began farming in the village.

The 1820s, 30s and 'hungry' 40s were a hard time for farmers, but those who improved their land and tried out the new crops and machinery which were becoming readily available managed to stay in business until the 1850s when farming became extremely profitable again. Land drainage was very important in Fulbourn and this was greatly aided by steam-powered machinery.

The Fulbourn farmers, despite differences of religious affiliation (in the first half of the century roughly half were Anglican and half nonconformist) worked together in close co-operation, running village affairs under the benevolent aegis of the Townley family. As major employers they dominated village society. They played cricket together, met for meals at the local inns and married each other's sons and daughters. When fires broke out in the village, as they frequently did, they were on hand to help before the 'engine' arrived from Cambridge. They encouraged the setting up of a National School and a Working Men's Institute, sponsored Sunday School treats, and engaged in other charitable activities; but this was a very paternalistic society, many farm labourers living close to the poverty line. As a result of this there was a lot of petty theft in the village, mainly of foodstuffs such as poultry. Although, compared to other areas, the local magistrates were reluctant to hand out harsh sentences, many young men were sentenced to hard labour, and sometimes to transportation, for relatively small crimes, leaving their wives and children to live off parish charity. Boys, and sometimes girls, worked long hours in the fields from an early age, often missing out on schooling in order to contribute a little extra to the family's meagre wages.

Another sad fact that we often forget is the high mortality rate among children and young people at this time. Henry Payne, who was farming in Fulbourn at the beginning of the nineteenth century, had twenty-four grandchildren, eight of whom died before they reached the age of twenty, and a further three did not reach the age of thirty-five. Among the families of farm labourers, who did not always have enough to eat, the mortality rate was probably higher.

However, many of the extracts from the Cambridge Chronicle show that the village was a place where people joined together to help each other and to celebrate, as they do today. The following passages illustrate this co-operative spirit:

10 January 1852

Fulbourn fire: A fire broke out at this village on Thursday night, on the premises of Mr Henry Hardwick, carrier... Mr Stephen Payne despatched a messenger to Cambridge for the engines, and the Royal Farmers' was despatched as quickly as possible; but on its arrival found that all danger was at an end, the fire having been subdued by the private engine of R.G. Townley, Esq., M.P., aided by the exertions of the inhabitants. The Norwich Union and the Phoenix engines were sent from Cambridge also, but not as quickly as might have been. The fire was confined to the tenement in which it originated, the building being partially destroyed. The furniture of the tenant was much damaged by removal. The fact of the building being on fire was first accounced by two passers-by named Page and Gifford; but we rejoice to state that there is but little doubt that the same was caused by the servant dropping a spark from a candle in the chamber in which it originated. The premises standing on the same site were burnt down in October 1851. The wind was blowing very strongly at the time, and it was fortunate that a mastery was obtained over the fire in time, or much damage would necessarily have resulted.

5 November 1853

Fulbourn Fete: On Tuesday last a subscription tea party was given to the Sunday School children of the parish of All Saints. The children, amounting to upwards of 100, assembled in the school room at 2 o'clock in the afternoon and marched in procession from thence to the place of entertainment, headed by their respective teachers, and carrying banners suitable to the occasion. When all the company had collected together, the children sat down to tea in a barn belonging to Mr Merington (one of the local farmers) which was beautifully decorated with festoons of flowers and evergreens, and hung round with banners and appropriate mottoes, presenting a most pleasing effect to the eye. The tables were tastefully laid out with towering bouquets of flowers and quantitities of rich plumb cake. On the children being settled the scene became truly animated, teachers and friends all vieing with each other in their attendance on the Sunday School scholars, who all seemed to enjoy the treat prepared for them. When their repast concluded the children adjourned to a field and amused themselves with various plays, such as cricket, bat and ball, &c. The teachers and a great number of guests then sat down and enjoyed "the cup that cheers but not inebriates". After the teachers and friends had partaken of their repast a brilliant display of fireworks was let off which added more life and enjoyment to the scene. The evening was concluded by all assembling in the barn where the thronged assembley were address by the Rev. Basil E. Aldwell (curate of the parish), Dr Hall and H.Thirling of Cambridge. At 9 o'clock the large party dispersed every one pleased wtih the entertainment, which all said was the greatest day Fulbourn had known in their recollection. Although the first day of dreary November, the sun shone out with unwonted brightness, and not a cloud marred the prospects of the day. Too much praise cannot be given to Mr and Mrs Merington, who conducted the entire arrangements on this interesting occasion.

Judy Hanmer

Reference: D Crane, Fulbourn Chronicles

Sunday Morning November 1881

My name is Elizabeth Mitchell but everyone calls me Betsy. I am 12 years old and I live with my mother, father and younger sisters Harriet and Mary in a little cottage in Stonebridge Lane. My big sister Jane doesn't live with us anymore as she is now in service at Six Mile Bottom. As today is mother's birthday her kind mistress has given her the whole day off so the family can be together.

It's Sunday morning and time to get ready for chapel. Really it's called the Congregational church but we call it the chapel so as not to get mixed up with the church of St Vigor. Mother is already putting on her best bonnet and shawl and father his Sunday cap; I am very excited because I have a new dress. The first new dress I ever had! It's as blue as the sky and no one has ever worn it before. Soon I will be going into service and I will wear the dress to meet the mistress of the house, so I must be sure not to get it dirty.

There's a swish of silk skirts as the richer ladies of the village take their places in their favourite pews. The gentlemen with fine whiskers and bright cravats follow them carrying their top hats. Pews can be reserved for sixpence a week. Last month a beautiful new schoolroom was added onto the side of the church on land given by Mr. Basil Chaplin. The hot pipes fed from the new coke boiler make the building warm and cosy.

The congregation stop chattering as the Reverend Moore in his flowing surplice goes up the steps to the pulpit. Next we stand to sing the first hymn. Miss Moore plays the organ while a boy from our lane does the pumping. He's paid two pence a week for this. I would like to earn two pence but the job always goes to a boy.

Now the sermon is beginning. Father says if I don't listen I will incur 'the wrath of God.' I'm not sure what this means but it sounds very frightening so I try very hard not to daydream. I wish I was back in the Sunday School with Mr. Sallows but now I'm twelve I'm too old. I loved listening to his exciting stories about Moses and the other prophets. I think he looks just like pictures of Moses with his long flowing beard and kind face.

It seems that the sermon this morning is going to be a very long one and although I try hard to concentrate I find myself thinking about other things. I remember the things that my granny told me about what the church was like when she was young.

She told me that the first chapel was built in 1810 when she was just a little girl. Before that dissenters, as they were called, met wherever they could in places like barns and sheds. Mr. Joseph Hancock, a gentleman farmer and regular attender at these meetings, could see that a proper building was needed. He paid for the first proper chapel to be built here in Home End. It was, at first, called 'The Dissenting Meeting House'. Mr. Joseph Chaplin was the first church member but soon many other people wanted to join and there wasn't enough room inside for everyone. The church was twice made bigger. Now there are usually about two hundred people at morning and evening services and over 100 members.

The Reverend Moore is coming down from the pulpit and I must stop daydreaming. We stand to sing the last hymn of the service 'Guide me O thou great redeemer', a favourite of mine so I sing loudly. After the blessing we go home for a special dinner to celebrate mother's birthday.

Footnote:

Church membership continued to rise well into the twentieth century and over the years various improvements were made to the building. In 1972 it became the Fulbourn United Reformed Church and in 1984 a legacy left by Miss Drury, a Sunday School leader for many years, enabled a new kitchen and meeting room to be added. In 1991 a complete refurbishment was carried out. The removal of the fixed pews and pulpit and their replacement chairs and staging made the use of the church more flexible. Also that year, as part of the 150th anniversary celebrations, the church received a visit from Lady Mary Wilson whose father the Reverend Baldwin was minister here in the 1920s.

Today the church has a small but loyal congregation. Services are still held every Sunday morning and in late 2010 Reverend Nigel Uden was appointed the new minister a position shared with the church of St Columba's in Cambridge.

Information taken from 'Fulbourn United Reformed Church' compiled by N.J Osborne and The Fulbourn Chronicles by D.J Crane

Iris Levitt

PM'S Wife from Fulbourn

From 1964 to 1970 and from 1974 to 1976 the Prime Minister of the United Kingdom was Harold Wilson. His wife Mary used to live in Fulbourn. Mary was born in 1918 and her father Rev Daniel Baldwin was Congregationalist Minister in Fulbourn from 1920 to 1926.

A union of the Congregational Church in England and Wales in 1972 and the Presbyterian Church of England produced the United Reformed Church (URC) across the country. And of course we have a United Reformed Church (URC) in Fulbourn.

Mary Wilson's father, as the Congregationalist minister, encouraged plain living and high thinking. Mary recalls "Church twice on Sundays and no novels to be read on the day of prayer". The family watchwords were "pride" and "propriety". Mary wrote much poetry, including one on the Fulbourn Manse.

One current Fulbourn resident had an uncle in the Cabinet. Today that resident has a daughter in the Cabinet Office working closely with the Deputy Prime Minister and other luminaries. But I guess only Mary Wilson from Fulbourn ended up living in No. 10 Downing Street.

Peter Godber

Fulbourn and Child Labour

Fulbourn occupies an important place in the history of child labour.

In the nineteenth century, young boys were often used by chimney sweeps to clean soot out of chimneys. Chimney sweeping was a job children could do better than adults. Small boys from the age of 5 with scrapers attached to their arms would be sent (often naked) scrambling up inside the chimney to scrape and brush soot away. When they got to the chimney pot at the top of the chimney, which could be as much as 60 feet from the ground, they were expected to shout out so that those below knew they had covered the whole chimney.

They regularly came down covered in soot, and with bleeding elbows and knees.

The chimneys were usually very narrow (in some cases as small as 30cm) and twisted. Children often got stuck or froze with terror in the cramped darkness - in these cases the Master Chimney Sweeper would simply light the fire underneath to 'encourage' them to get on with their work.

The work was dangerous and painful. Some boys got stuck and died of suffocation. If they fell on the way down, some of them suffocated in the enormous pile of soot they had scraped off and which was now at the foot of the chimney

In the early 19th century the House of Lords threw out attempts to make the use of climbing boys illegal. “Our mansions may catch fire if our chimneys are not swept” was their attitude No compassion there.

A change in the law was achieved but boys were still illegally used for sweeping chimneys in large houses. And then an event in Fulbourn changed things.

George Brewster was an eleven-year-old boy who was probably the last boy to die as a result of climbing a chimney. And it was in Fulbourn. He died in 1875 sweeping a chimney at Fulbourn Hospital. He was apprenticed to William Wyer who had the contract to sweep the flues of three boilers at Fulbourn Hospital, Cambridge, three times a year.

George went into a flue of which the door was twelve inches by six. In about a quarter of an hour he was pulled out in an exhausted state. A doctor was summoned. He found George Brewster alive and he removed the soot from his mouth. The doctor gave him brandy and put him in a warm bath, but he died in a short time. A *post mortem* examination revealed that his arms were “abraded”, his head “congested”, and there was much black powder in his lungs and windpipe.

The George Brewster incident was publicised and Lord Shaftesbury, the great social reformer wrote letters to the Times. He then presented a Bill to Parliament. The Bill became law. It was enforceable. It stopped the practice of sending boys up chimneys.

The Fulbourn incident had a dreadful outcome for George Brewster. It did though have a pivotal place in the process of bringing to an end the appalling scandal of child labour.

Peter Godber

Reference: 1996 Clarke, David H ‘The Story of a mental hospital: Fulbourn 1858-1983’

Almsgiving and Charity in the parishes of St Vigor's and All Saints, Fulbourn

A Cardinal Virtue and Christian Duty; the distribution of alms to the poor and needy can be traced back to the very beginnings of the Christian Church. The pagan virtues discoursed on by the Greek philosophers of prudence, justice, temperance and fortitude (Plato, The Republic), were adapted for Christianity by the early Church Fathers. Chief among these were St. Thomas Aquinas (Summa Theologica), St. Augustine of Hippo (De Civitate Dei), and St Ambrose (Letters), (www.newadvent.org;The Catholic Encyclopaedia).

Aquinas, when translating the Greek texts into Latin, combined the theological virtues of faith, hope and charity with the four pagan virtues to produce the Christian Cardinal virtues. In his teachings Aquinas held that though charity and compassion for another was a spontaneous product of mercy and a sense of justice, the virtue of mercy was a special virtue in itself. Over time the Scholastics, (among them Anselm of Canterbury, Duns Scotus and William of Ockham (www.newadvent.org; The Catholic Encyclopaedia), considered it within the framework of justice because justice could be catalogued as a distinct set of controls and obligations which regulated relations between certain groups and individuals. The needs of others could be both temporal and spiritual;

- The traditional Corporal works of Mercy are to feed the hungry; to give drink to the thirsty; to clothe the naked; to harbour the harbourless; to visit the sick; to ransom the captive; and to bury the dead.
- The Spiritual works of Mercy are to instruct the ignorant; to counsel the doubtful; to admonish sinners; to bear wrongs patiently; to forgive offences willingly; to comfort the afflicted; and to pray for the living and the dead; (www.newadvent.org; The Catholic Encyclopaedia)

The virtue that concerns us here is charity, which was translated from the Greek word agape, (which means selfless love) into the Latin word caritas and thence to the English translation charity.

Charity, the giving of alms to the poor, was regarded as a Christian duty for all and the sacred texts enjoin Christians again and again to be charitable to the less well off.

Love of God was equated with love of man. When Jesus was asked by the Pharisees which was the most important Commandment he replied 'Love thy God with thy whole heart and thy whole soul and love thy neighbour as thyself' (1Cor13). The message is repeated over and over, 'Ye cannot serve God and Mammon'; 'Lay not up for yourselves treasures on earth ...but lay up for yourselves treasures in heaven'; 'Blessed art the poor for they shall inherit the earth'. This rather revolutionary concept frightened the rich and gave hope to the poor.

The motivation for almsgiving varied. For some it was abiding by the law of God as preached in the Bible. For others who had perhaps not lived blameless lives, the motive was the redemptive qualities of the giving of alms, which was seen as an almost compensatory act for previous sins or shortcomings. The tension between piety and guilt has a long history.

Charity in England before the 20th Century. In the Anglo-Saxon church the tradition of almsgiving was well established. St. Bede in his Ecclesiastical History records St. Aidan praising King Oswald of Northumbria for his charity to the poor. The early churches and monasteries and later the parish churches encouraged the better off to donate money and goods to be dispensed among the poor.

By the late medieval period the crown had enacted a system of Poor Laws. The continuing growth in population and the dissolution of the monasteries at the time of the Reformation, led to a reduction in charitable almsgiving. The Tudors under Elizabeth I changed the Old Poor Laws and codified them 1587-1597. In the allocation of relief a distinction was made between the deserving and the undeserving poor or shiftless and feckless. With industrialisation and the consequent shift of population from rural to urban the need for an improved centrally administered system of poor relief became necessary. In 1834 the Victorians enacted the New Poor Laws. Administrative bodies known as the Poor Law Unions were set up and Workhouses to house the indigent were built in the towns and cities. The poor did not see the workhouse as a refuge but as a last resort and the thought of 'ending up in the poorhouse' has lived on in the folk memory of the people as being a fate worse than death.

At parish level both in rural and urban areas the church continued in what had been its traditional role and one of its most important functions. The services of the Church in the relief of poverty, social, educational and medical care, were still very much in demand. The group of people at parish level who administered this were the local squire or lord of the manor, the parson, the churchwarden and the schoolmaster. This group constituted what is still known as the Parish Council (The History of Parish Councils; www.whetstone.org.uk).

Fulbourn Wills and Endowments. The village of Fulbourn was well endowed with charities from c15th. In 1442 John Careway, priest of St Vigor's, invested in approximately 100 acres to pay parliamentary fifteenths (a crown tax) for the poorer people of the parish, that is, people with an acrage of 40 or less who could not afford to pay the tax without selling some of their land. Surplus income was to be disposed of in charitable gifts to the poor by the parish. The land included both closes (partially enclosed areas within the precincts of a church) and arable land. After Enclosure in the 1730s fifty-eight and a half acres continued to be arable land yielding rent. The remainder of the land was divided into plots of between a quarter and one acre plots and rented to the landless labourers of the parish. The plots yielded rents, which increased from £23 per annum in the early 18th century to £150 by the 1890's.

In 1474 the priest Geoffrey Bishop of All Saints parish left £63 in his will to be disbursed on requiem masses for his soul, Peter's Pence, an annual collection for the Pope collected on the Sunday nearest the feast day of Saints Peter and Paul and on the Ely Farthings, an annual collection for the Bishop of Ely. At the time of the enclosures 83 acres, known as Bishops Charity Farm was let for charitable purposes.

Incomes yielded from these endowments were used to pay tax, rates, clothing and material for clothing. Later in the 19th century the money was used for gift vouchers to be redeemed in local shops, a coal club, support for almshouses, pensioners and loaves given out at Christmas and Easter.

The Richard Wright Clock Land Charity was founded sometime before 1525. It was set up to ensure the continuation of the ringing of the curfew bell and the day bell, and the repair and maintenance of the tower, the steeple, the clock and the bell of St Vigor's Church. The original endowment of 23 acres of land was exchanged after enclosure in the 18th century for 14 acres, 2 roods and 34 perches of land. The annual rent accrues from the property are used to pay for the costs of the bell tower. The land is situated at the Tesco roundabout on the left side of the Cambridge road from Fulbourn. (115-208 Search Catalogue; www.Calm.Cambridgeshire.gov.uk ....Archives Catalogue).

In 1712 William Farmer of Fulbourn decreed in his will that on the event of his widow's death, his estates were to be sold and that the proceeds were to be invested to pay doles for the poor of All Saints who were 'constant' churchgoers. From the 1750's the income from this bequest was allocated in weekly doles after church services to between ten and twenty people. The Parish Council chose the recipients individually. From the 1820's onwards the recipients were chosen by 'emborisation'. That is, names were drawn off a set list from a purse or bursa. It was thought that this might improve church attendance.

In 1722 Thomas Oslar left £12 in his will to buy land to endow an annual dole for 'the poor widows of St Vigor's '. The 'widow's acre' yielded ten shillings by 1751 and £2 by 1780. From 1780-1840 the doles were given to between six and ten widows and these payments continued into the 1990's.

In her will of 1722 Elizabeth March of the Farmer family endowed land at Oakington (worth £70 by 1780) for the free education of poor children in five Cambridgeshire parishes including Fulbourn. Prior to this schooling had been provided by the curates of the parish, schoolmasters and dame schools. The March endowment, together with voluntary contributions was used to set up and run March's school until the 1880s. After the Education Act providing free education for all children from five to thirteen years under School Boards, a new school was built in Fulbourn.

A group of eleven cottages, described in 1800 as almshouses, stood on the north side of the graveyard. These may have been the Town houses described in a document of 1666 (P.R.O., E 179/244/22, f.83). The cottages were not endowed with any income for repair and maintenance so that by 1860s they were very dilapidated and virtually uninhabitable. They were demolished in 1864 and eight new brick cottages were built on a site across the road given by C.W. Townley of Fulbourn. Places were given to old age pensioners of good character. In 1931 H.F. Chaplin of Fulbourn left £1000 in his will to be used for the repair and maintenance of the almshouses and to provide pocket money for the residents.

In 1901 Ellen Weston, a widow of the village, gave twelve cottages for the poor of St Vigors. Rents were charged at £60-80 per annum and this money was distributed in the form of vouchers until 1910. The houses were sold in the 1920's and the income of £22-32 was given to the poor. This was discontinued in the 1960's when there were 20 beneficiaries.

Present day Charity and Support in the Fulbourn Community. The Victorian Poor Laws carried on until they were largely abolished in 1948 with the passing of the National Assistance Act. This heralded the beginning of the Welfare State. At first not all benefits were universal and were means tested but as the 20th century progressed many benefits became universal. In the 21st century with changing demographics and the spiralling cost of benefits, means testing has been increased.

Meanwhile the parish charities continue with their ancient endowments, which are now used for a variety of grants for practical and educational needs. With greater prosperity, population growth and changing demographics the needs of the community and the parish have changed. There is a significant increase in the number of services, societies and clubs for both young and old in the village. Volunteers run most of these activities. In 2006 the Townley Memorial Hall, The Fulbourn Sports and Social Club was refurbished and extended and serves the community as a meeting place for clubs, meetings and entertainment for the people of the village. The recreation ground, which covers 16 acres, is used for a variety of sports and outdoor activities. Fulbourn Nature Reserve situated to the east of the manor house is an area of outstanding beauty and charm. It includes a number of different habitats containing many species of wild plants. There is woodland, scrub and meadow. Much of the meadowland is an SSSI (Site of Special Scientific Interest) which has never been ploughed or treated with herbicide, pesticide or fertilizers.

Villagers are proactive in providing community services that cannot be provided by local government. Two notable recent examples of this include the takeover of Fulbourn Library from Cambridgeshire County Council by volunteers and the provision of day centre services and a lunch club for the over 65s. People in Fulbourn continue to donate both time and money to village, local, national and international charities.

Maire Jagger

The Railway

When I first moved to Fulbourn in 1979 I lived in Station Road, just four houses down from the level crossing where a single, somewhat derelict, platform was the only indication that there had once been a station there. Small two-carriage trains still went along the single track about every three hours, often with just two or three passengers on their way between Cambridge and Ipswich. There must have been a busier time for this spot, I thought, and indeed there was. Using the Fulbourn Village History Society's records, I decided to find the story of Fulbourn's Railways.

My first surprise was that this station was not the earliest to serve the village; that had been located about half a mile from the village centre on the Balsham Road, on a line long since removed. Eileen Beeton of Home Farm's memoirs included stories of her family using this station to collect coal for their delivery business. Why had there been two railways built so close together? Uncovering the timing of construction of the railways reveals a period of somewhat chaotic expansion (see plan).

The mid nineteenth century saw major developments in railways throughout the country, and the Eastern Counties Railway Company completed the line from Bishopsgate in London to Cambridge and Ely in 1845. The East Anglian Railway company built lines from Kings Lynn and Norwich about the same time, and links were planned by both between Newmarket, Norwich, Peterborough and Cambridge. Careful planning does not seem to have been a strong point of the Eastern Counties company. The first part of their local extensions was to Newmarket, leaving the London line at Chesterford. This was started in 1846 but progress was marred by a series of accidents and work stopped in 1847. Construction started again the next year and the line was soon in use, with the link from Cambridge to Newmarket also begun. But then financial difficulties led the Company's shareholders to sack the whole Board of Directors and both lines were not finally completed, under new management, till 1851. Fulbourn's new station was officially opened in October that year, with two tracks and two platforms; sidings for loading freight; waiting room and ticket-office; Station-Master's house; signal box; and the essential crossing gates. Once this line was in use, the Chesterford to Newmarket line ceased to operate, becoming one of the country's first railway closures at the end of 1851.

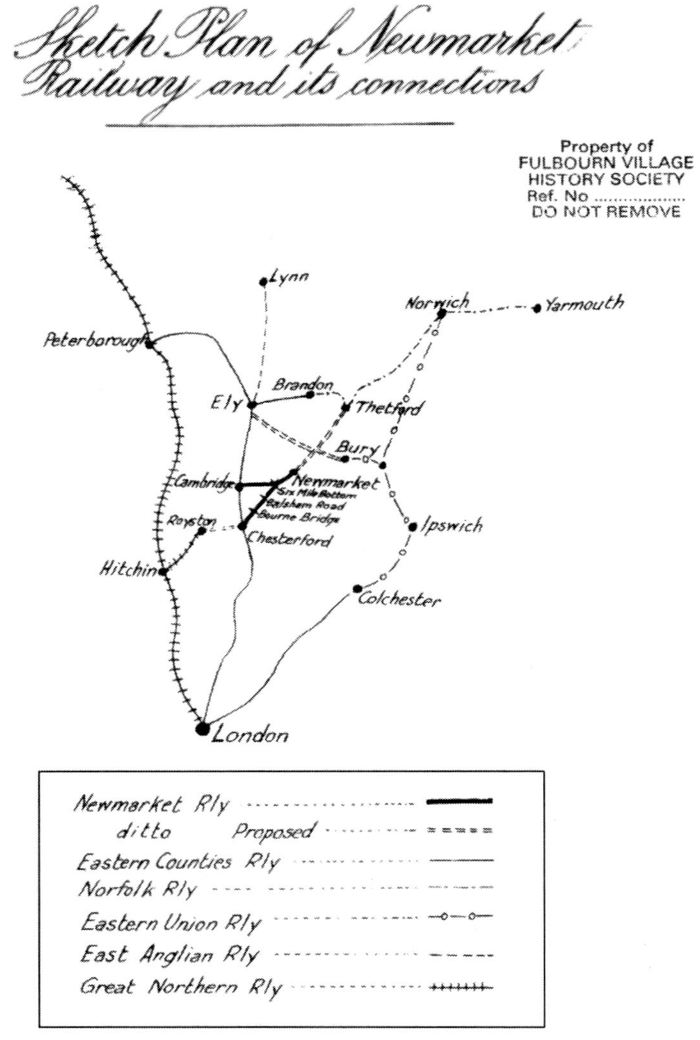

Plan showing Fulbourn's first station on Balsham Road
Date unknown – probably 1845-1850

East Anglia's railways eventually re-grouped into the Great Eastern Railway Company in 1923, then into the London and North Eastern Railways, and in 1948 into British Railways. It was Dr Beeching's famous (or infamous, depending on your view) Government Report of 1963 that led to the closure of Fulbourn's Station in 1966.

Once in use, Fulbourn's Station was an important place of employment. Station Masters were figures of some authority, appointed by the Railway Company, supplied with a house, and often moved from station to station. They wore an official uniform, always with a gold-braided cap. I haven't found who the first Station Master was at Fulbourn, but the second one was certainly no model employee. On December 15th 1855, it's reported that Mr Benjamin Richardson had absconded, and the Railway Books were under investigation. He had only been Station Master for eight months, and had a wife and eight children. But the next appointment was perhaps more characteristic of the post. He was Thomas Riches and was in Fulbourn for 21 years, before being moved to Welnetham. He died in 1886 after 40 years working for the railways. Charles Parsons and Ernest Orman followed, both serving long periods, and then in 1927 Mr S. T. Beales took over. In May 1929 he was moved on to Fordham – Fulbourn's loss, it seems, as it was reported that *"During this time he has transformed the station, and its picturesque aspect has been much admired."* In 1940 Mr J. Hussey filled the post, then Mr D. G. White from 1952-63, and the last occupier of the Station House was Mr A. Crane.

Under the Station Master were porters, ticket-collectors, signalmen and gate-keepers. Mostly these would have lived in a local railway-owned house next to the line. Safety on the railways did not have the same attention as it does today, as an incident in 1901 shows. In December that year, Edward Hart, a 60 year-old farm labourer, was killed at the crossing on Teversham Road at about 8pm. The night was misty, and on passing through the crossing, the engine driver felt a bump and stopped his train. His mate walked back and found the dead man on the line, with a broken gate across it, and significantly, no light on the gate. What should have happened is that the gatekeeper, William Nicholls, would have opened the gates for the train on receiving a signal from the station, with an oil lamp on the gate to warn everyone of its presence. Where was Mr Nicholls? Found in the Bakers' Arms, where according to his statement given later, he had gone to find something to treat his diarrhoea! It was unlawful for Mr Nicholls to leave his post, and he should not have asked his neighbour Mr Hart to stand in for him; so he was found guilty of manslaughter at the inquest. When the case came before the Cambridge Spring Assizes, the Jury found him 'guilty of feloniously killing Edward Hart' but recommended mercy, and the Judge decided not to pass any sentence. The case is fully reported in the Fulbourn Chronicle for January 1902, and ends with – "This decision was received with applause in Court". I doubt the same conclusion would be reached today!

A second case was reported in January 1922, when a youth of 15 years, son of the Fulbourn gatekeeper at that time, was killed while working at Six Mile Bottom Station. His name was Reginald Willie Whitehouse, and he had been assisting shunting operations on the sidings. At the inquest, his duties were outlined as *'confined to the platform and waiting rooms, with the addition of the lamps and gates'*. His father complained that he had not been told his son was helping with shunting operations, but the porter at Six Mile Bottom said that *'boys anxious to get on often did jobs voluntarily'*. The verdict was accidental death with no blame attached to anyone. There were numerous other fatal accidents on the line between Newmarket and Cambridge, particularly at the crossings, and it was not until the 1980's that all these were automated.

Who and what used the railways? Much of their early importance must have been in carrying freight before such things as heavy lorries existed ; coal, building materials, agricultural produce, even horses from the Newmarket Stables, were all carried by rail. The earliest train of the day took the post and papers along the line, and there are reports that occasionally, this train FORGOT to stop at Fulbourn! Gradually the possibilities for passenger travel also grew, and single day excursions were advertised to London, Ipswich and Harwich (the latter by boat), Cromer, or Yarmouth. The costs for such excursions were 6 to 8 shillings in the first class enclosed carriages, and exactly half that in the open-sided canvas-roofed cars.

Some started even longer journeys from Fulbourn Station, and in July 1854, there is a report of much *'excitement and confusion'* as 250 people turned up to witness the departure of some 30 emigrants setting off on the long journey to Australia. They were not the only ones – in April 1855, the day after their marriage in Fulbourn, Henry Outlaw and Ann Ison set off with another couple for Sydney, Australia. There were *"touching scenes"* at the Station as their families said farewell to the young people setting out for their new life.

Probably most journeys were much shorter – to Cambridge for the market, Newmarket for the Races, and perhaps the occasional commuter used the train for work in Cambridge or even London. A single ticket to Cambridge cost just 8 old pence, and in November 1855 two young Fulbourn girls ended up before Bottisham Magistrates for trying to avoid this. Sarah Ann Littlechild and Esther Hawkes walked to Cambridge one Sunday, took the train home and were met on the Station by Mr Riches' young son, who collected two tickets from them. When his father looked at these, he realised they were halves of two old tickets, so father and son set off into the village where the two girls were soon identified and charged with travelling without paying their fare. At the Bottisham Court, Esther Hawkes pleaded guilty and was fined 5 shillings + expenses of 11s 6d, but Sarah Ann still maintained her ticket was valid, and was therefore fined the same amount plus an extra 2 shillings (roughly equivalent to £66 today) for refusing to admit her guilt.

When the station opened, there were just 4 trains each way from Monday to Saturday, slightly less on a Sunday. In the next timetable I've found - June 1930 - 8 trains went along the line daily each way, some of which were through trains to London, taking just over two hours with only one stop at Cambridge before continuing to Liverpool Street. In 1963, when the Beeching Report was published, 20 diesel-powered trains went each way, carrying freight (coal, grain and sugarbeet) and/or passengers. So why was the station scheduled for closure?

The increase in road transport began having a serious effect on rail use in the post-2ndWW years; at the same time, the extensive rail network built up in the nineteenth century was in dire need of modernisation. The two factors led to a serious imbalance in the finances of British Railways, and the then Conservative Transport Minister Ernest Marples commissioned the Report. Beeching believed there was a strong future for a highly modernised system between the main cities, but that the public service element of rail travel should be cut. Many rural lines and smaller stations were therefore scheduled for closure. In the event, it was the Labour Transport Minister Barbara Castle who set a date for Fulbourn's closure, and despite protests from the local MP and many others, the last scheduled train to stop at Fulbourn pulled in at 9.05pm on New Year's Eve, 1966. The Cambridge Evening News reported that four people got out, one the reporter, the others - a man, a small boy and a woman, who *"hurried away into the darkness and the cold, apparently unmoved by this latest stroke of the Beeching Axe."*

So what happened to the buildings associated with the station? These were not all owned by British Railways. A public house, the Railway Tavern, had opened on Station Road around 1870, and had been used by those waiting for passengers or delivery of freight. But its use had declined in the 50s, and it closed around 1960. The building remained derelict for some time before being demolished. The Station house and ticket office remained for some years too, and can be seen in the background of a photo in 1973, when a special train stopped at the platform to pick up the entire population of the Village School for an excursion to Ely. That event is the subject of a film held in the History Society Archive. The old station yard was taken over by a garage at about that time, and although some of the buildings were used at first, a big fire in 1980 cleared these, to leave nothing but the small Waiting Room by the remaining platform on the Cambridge side of the line. This was pulled down in 2002.

Special Train to Ely at Fulbourn Station, 1973
photo: Cambridge Newspapers

Could the railway ever serve the Village again? Would it be used if the station were re-opened? I believe this has been explored and so far rejected, but I am unable to find any relevant papers. Currently 8 trains a day run along the single track each way. Most of Fulbourn's households own at least one car, and there is a reasonable bus service into Cambridge. But as oil prices rise and supplies decline, other forms of transport will need to be explored. Perhaps this easy, direct route into Cambridge could be reviewed again.

Gill Aslett

Reference: ed. D Crane 'Fulbourn Chronicles', Keith Osborne 'The Railway Comes to Ely'; all held at Fulbourn Village History Society

Fulbourn Voluntary Aid Detachment Hospital, 1914-1918

The National Schoolroom in Fulbourn[1] was built in 1859 at the cost of £624 to educate children between the ages of 5-12. With the terrible slaughter of servicemen in France and Belgium, the need for convalescent hospitals became urgent, and the Rev'd C.F.Townley of Fulbourn Manor, County Director of the Red Cross, asked if there were any buildings suitable for use as a Voluntary Aid Detachment (V.A.D.) Hospital. In November 1914, the Rector of Fulbourn, the Rev'd J.V. Durrell, gave permission for the Church of England Infants School and Meeting Room to be used.

In four days the entire Infants School moved to the Congregational Church Hall and stayed there until November 1918. The older children continued to be taught in their classrooms at the National School.

The Church School made an entire and compact Red Cross Hospital. The accommodation was as follows: entering the lobby, on the left was a large and lofty ward (the school Assembly Room) which held seventeen beds, with two open fire grates; attached to this ward was the bathroom and washroom. In a second lobby was a large boiler, taken over from the Welsh Division, with water laid on by the Rev'd Townley. Opening out from the large ward was the nurses' private kitchen. Beyond this was the second ward, originally the infants' classroom, which held eleven beds; opening out from here was a storeroom that became the larder, with a wire door fitted so that it was nice and airy. In the passage between the two wards, a kitchen was fitted with two cooking stoves, water tank, and convenient shelving. Here all the cooking was done, with the exception of the large meat joints which were kindly cooked by the village baker, Mr Ellis.

[1]The remaining old school building on School Lane, now owned by the County Council and unused since the Library moved out, is only part of the original, part of the school was demolished for the old library to be built. More information and photos available in the History Society Archive.

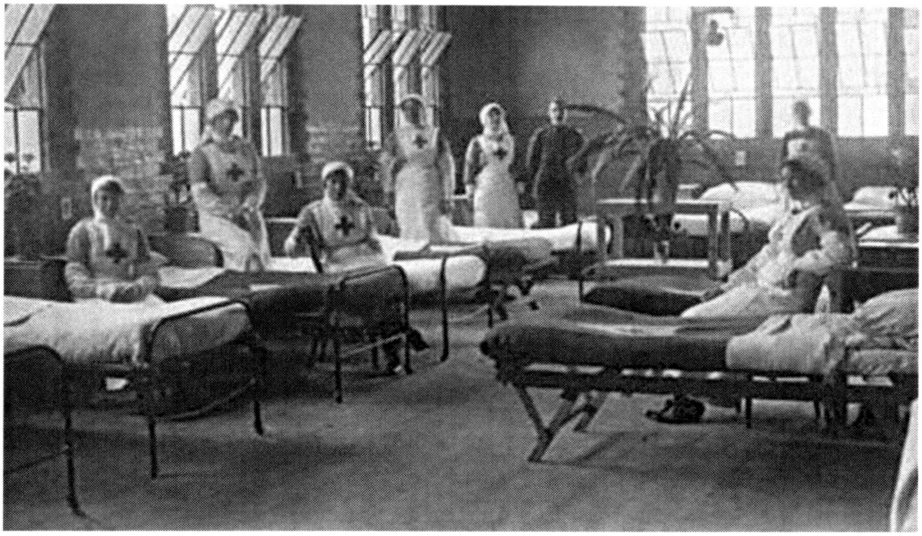

Fulbourn's VAD Hospital, 1914

The Hospital was connected by a temporary covered way to outhouses used for washing up purposes, storing coal etc. These were part of the Fulbourn Institute and Reading-room, closed for the duration of the war. The Institute made an ideal mess-room and recreation room for the patients, and was provided with a billiard table, piano and library.

Dr Nicholls, the local doctor, headed the medical staff. On the 27th November 1914 a meeting was called in the village to form a V.A.D. for men to relieve the nurses at night and to help with the transportation of patients. Forty men volunteered their services.

In the period between 1914-18 Fulbourn V.A.D. Hospital helped to bring back to health 1,378 servicemen. The Hospital closed on the 30th November 1918 and the infants school moved back into their premises.

Norman Osborne

Miss Dorothy G Nicholls 1886-1980

The daughter of Fulbourn's local doctor, Miss Nicholls took a diploma as a dispenser of medicines when she left the Perse girls school, although in those days parents did not approve of girls earning their own living. When 18 years old, she went to a children's hospital in Brighton and in later life found this opportunity of studying children and young people invaluable. Miss Nicholls then went to St Georges Hospital, London, to train as a State Registered Nurse and on completing her training, returned to Brighton to qualify in Midwifery.

She completed her training as war broke out in 1914 and volunteered to go to France with the Red Cross to nurse wounded soldiers. With a handful of nurses they took over the sugar sheds in Boulogne docks, turned them into a hospital and with a few beds and little equipment, began nursing the soldiers being brought down from the front line. Previously the men were shipped straight back to England with very little attention. Miss Nicholls had 100 stretchers to look after with only the help of a few orderlies. After working for several months at a terrific pace with inadequate equipment and little sleep, she left with a few colleagues to tend to Belgian civilians suffering from typhoid fever in a small town near the fighting. The Army wanted the nurses to join them but they returned to England after six months in France.

Miss Nicholls then volunteered to go to Russia to nurse the wounded. She left when the Baltic was closed, so had to go in at Archangel and was on the last boat to get through before the water became frozen over. During the time in Russia, she helped to convert a palace into a hospital, and went to the Russian front with a field hospital which organised a casualty clearing hospital in the south. It was while visiting the Carpathian front that Miss Nicholls was awarded the St George Medal, given at the time to troops in the firing line. When the revolution began in 1917 they had to leave and on returning to England she became a night sister at the Military Hospital at Epsom. When the war finally ended she became Matron of the Marlborough Maternity Hospital at Endsleigh Street, London from 1918-1921. Under supervision it became a training school for nurses working to get their midwifery qualifications and she started one of the first infant welfare and ante-natal clinics in London. But it was not long before Miss Nicholls was abroad again. This time working for the Lady Muriel Paget's Mission in the Baltics. She worked in the three republics, Estonia, Latvia and Lithuania, starting child welfare clinics.

It was in 1923 when she came back to Fulbourn to nurse her mother, after whose death she settled down in her own village to keep home for her father. All her achievements during 94 years of life are too numerous to include, but briefly, she was a member of the Chesterton Rural District Council (Board of Guardians), was the first woman to be appointed to the Bottisham Magistrates, later becoming the first woman member of the Cambridgeshire Standing Joint Council Committee.

For 30 years she was a Manager and Correspondent of the Fulbourn Primary School, was a County Councillor for twelve years, and Visitor on the Committee of Fulbourn Hospital and member of Fulbourn Management Committee.

As chairman of the Bottisham Magistrates and a member of the Licensing Committee, she was keenly interested in the need for a general improvement in licensed houses in the Bottisham Petty Sessional Division.

Norman Osborne

'Jerusalem' and The Smiths

If you went along Cambridge Road in the sixties you would nearly always see a patient from Fulbourn Hospital wandering along, with or without clothes, with or without shoes. Sometimes they would make it to Cambridge or Fulbourn and eventually someone would come from the hospital, pick them up and take them back. If you visited the hospital you would see women on their hands and knees scrubbing the corridors like automatons. Later these were replaced by paid staff who came from Europe and Asia, to work in all trades at the hospital. These recruits lived in hospital accommodation but, if they got married, they needed homes of their own.

The need for social housing in Fulbourn was great at that time and the Parish Council allowed an experimental estate of quick build concrete houses to be erected on a field that they bought from the Church. The houses were grey with flat roofs, a square aspect and by some were considered unsightly. As a result the area was quickly nicknamed 'Jerusalem'

Some of the foreign workers married English people (no cohabiting in those days, or not openly at any rate) and moved into homes on the estate. Over the years many moved away, but one couple remained and this is their story.

Connie, a very attractive Italian from near Naples, was 20 in 1959. She was unhappy with the restrictions to her life caused by her Catholic upbringing and her dictatorial father, who believed in the traditional Italian way of life, resulting in little freedom for young women. She decided to leave home and get a job. When her Italian friend who had lived in England for some years, went back to Italy for a holiday, she told her about Fulbourn Hospital. They chatted about England and Connie thought this would suit her and be an ideal way to escape to a new life.

When she returned to England Connie's friend arranged for application forms to be sent to her. Within a short while Connie received a permit to come to Fulbourn Hospital and work as a Domestic. A forward-thinking doctor had arrived at Fulbourn Hospital and made great changes. Patients were no longer needed to work.

When she arrived the Immigration Office told Connie her papers were not valid and she had to spend the night at Customs. However, the next day the Matron came back from her holiday and said she still needed her. Connie made lots of friends while living in the Nurses' Home. After eight months her English had become fluent and she was offered training to become a State Enrolled Nurse.

Meanwhile, Ian had also left his parents' home in Romsey, Southampton and taken a job in Haverhill with Pye Telecomm, living in hotels and going back home at weekends. However, a chance meeting with a Virginian lad who was returning to America, led to his moving into 'digs' with an Italian lady in Haverhill. When he went home to see his mother he said he was moving in with an Italian lady and her English husband. She said: 'Now, don't go getting mixed up with no 'talian girls.' Little did Ian or his mother know what the future held in store.

Some months after he moved in, his landlady's sister asked him to go to a party at the Nurses' Home in Fulbourn Hospital. He went with four of his mates and met Connie. One of his friends, Peter, met Maria, and they all started going out together. Ian and Connie fell in love and so did Maria and Peter.

Ian and Connie wanted to get married and therefore Ian wanted to move to Cambridge. Pye didn't want to let him go, so he applied for a different job in Cambridge as a Test Engineer, which paid him £1000 pa compared with the £786 he had been getting (a good wage for the 1960s). They married in April 1966 and moved into a shared house. They put their names down on the waiting list for a council house with Cambridge City and South Cambs.

After three or four months they were offered one of the houses on the Windmill Estate. These houses were made available to nursing staff from Fulbourn and Addenbrookes Hospitals and as Connie was a Nurse she was offered one. They chose their house because it was south facing, the garden was the right size for them and they moved in, in October 1966.

The Smith's house

It was the beginning of the video-age and Ian soon got a job with his own workshop, designing security systems, cameras on operating microscopes and close circuit television systems for training for many different authorities, eg education, police, fire brigade and the university.

He installed a weather satellite dish on his roof, along with amateur radio masts and satellite television dish. These did not go unnoticed by his neighbours who were concerned about the 'scrap-yard in the sky' but he eventually got permission from the Council for his equipment to remain. Before his retirement he worked for the Pathology Department on the Downing Site in Cambridge as Deputy

Workshop Manager with his own electronics repair workshop. With his specialist knowledge in electronic engineering he was very valued. When he retired he looked forward to a happy life walking his dog.

But South Cambs District Council deemed otherwise.

Ian and Connie had bought their house freehold as part of the Right to Buy scheme in 1980. They expected to stay there until the end of their days. They have two daughters and extended their house, adding a substantial dining/living room and two extra bedrooms and they landscaped their garden. Connie continued to nurse at Fulbourn Hospital until she retired.

Early in the 21st century many of the houses on the Windmill Estate had begun to look neglected and there were no tenant charters or agreements invoked by South Cambridgeshire, who subsequently were looking at ways to save money. In 2003 negotiations started between Fulbourn Parish Council and South Cambs Rural District Council, to hand the estate over to a housing association. After an exhibition by five potential associations, Accent Nene was chosen to redevelop the estate and proposed the following choices:

1. Accent Nene to manage the estate without changes, but obviously the rents would go up, and there would be a service charge.

2. Partial redevelopment of the estate, ie building some rentable homes and new homes for sale, the money from which would be used towards the upkeep of the remaining part of the estate.

3. Treat it as a brown field site, knock it all down and build new homes, again a mixture of rentable and homes for sale.

Accent Nene then held meetings with the existing residents of the estate to assess their requirements for the new homes, and the residents were told they could have like for like, including any improvements eg downstairs toilet. However, when Ian pointed out that surely the new houses would be worth more than the existing houses, he was told that this was called 'shared equity', ie Ian would own the value of his property and Nene would own the other share. When Ian pointed out that this was not like for like, as he owned his house outright, he was told that he could not make a profit out of the housing association. Following this he pointed out that the houses that were being built were far smaller than the existing houses with regards to room sizes and land area.

At an early Council meeting the question was asked whether the houses described were really village houses - with gardens front and back and garage, like those in School Lane. Accent Nene also wanted to include three storey blocks of flats. The Parish Councillors said three storey flats had no place in a village. However, with the passing of the years and changes in the Council, and increasing housing need, they have obviously changed their minds.

Cambridge News published an article saying 75% of the residents of the Windmill Estate voted for new homes. Ian challenged this, as it was 75% of the tenants, not 75% of the residents because the residents were not asked to vote. Ian subsequently heard that 52% of that 75%, were on subsistence and when they learnt there would be an increase in rent under the housing association they complained and were told that was okay as they could put in an extra claim for the increase.

Naturally, who would not want a free new home.

Originally there were 168 homes on the estate. Nene initially proposed building 220 homes and on their website this was increased to 250 homes. Accent Nene negotiated with the Council and it was agreed that if they were allowed to build on the old infant school site (which had subsequently been used as a community centre when the infant school combined with the junior school) they would provide a new library, community centre, and health centre and then they could build 276 homes. The PCT did not want a new health centre so Accent Nene instead of reducing the number of homes, decided to build additional blocks of flats. Originally the number proposed for the area was 42 homes per hectare. However, the Planning Officer at that time did not agree insisting on more open spaces, more green areas and this number was reduced to 36 per hectare. This applied to phase 1A. The first phase was supposed to show what the estate was going to look like. The architects were asked to look at other houses in the village and to bring a village feel to the estate. They looked at the High Street, and various other areas and incorporated staggered houses with dormer windows, resulting in houses which look nothing like village houses. They are very tall compared with the rest of the houses in the village. Unfortunately the original Planning Officer has retired. The people in power just want more and more houses, with smaller and smaller gardens and less open spaces.

A Residents' Association was formed with tenants and owner-occupiers to protect the people and their homes. Some of the owner-occupiers and tenants wanted to stay in their homes, but one by one they changed their minds and now only a few remain.

Ian was told that if he did not move they would knock down the houses either side of him. Ian spoke to Bison, the company who built the original houses. They told him that the blocks were keyed together at the foundations, the first floor and roof. At the joints, there is an infill of concrete that was made on site, and there was no guarantee as to the quality of the concrete between the various blocks of houses. Even if you could knock down one house from one block it would not necessarily apply to other blocks on the estate.

Later Accent Nene's spokesperson said that they were going to get an expert in to find out how to remove independent houses from a block, so they could knock down the ones either side of Ian. On Grandridge Close they attempted to detach the end block but were unsuccessful and the whole block fell down.

Some residents of the village said that they had understood that the houses would have a limited life, maybe 12 to 15 years. Ian questioned Bison as to the life of the houses and was assured that they were good for at least 50 years, if not more.

Every time Ian went to one of the meetings, he was asked why he would not consider shared equity. He replied that it was because he did not have shared equity – he owned his home freehold and everything was to his liking. This was why he was not prepared to move.

Ian contacted South Cambs and Nene and said that if he received any further requests to take shared equity, he would regard this as harassment. Subsequently, South Cambs got advice from their solicitors and were told that he was indeed being harassed, and Accent Nene must keep him informed of all the developments regarding the estate, which they did.

Ian and Connie bought their house in good faith and felt no compulsory purchase orders should be made. Several of the other owner-occupiers had initially felt the same but had ultimately decided that they were going to seek other accommodation, not on the estate.

After a long battle Ian and Connie finally got a letter to say their block could remain. There has been some tongue in cheek talk of getting a preservation order on the block as a reminder of this type of house, which was part of Fulbourn for nearly fifty years.

Ian says: "An Englishman's home is his castle. When you have done everything you want to your home why should you have to start again?" He asks the question: "When is freehold not freehold? When a Housing Association takes over the site."

Connie has had some hurtful remarks from people because she prefers to remain in her flat roofed home rather than moving to a new (smaller) house. But, as she says, she was brought up in a flat roofed house, as in Italy this is the norm!

Jill Woolley

Personal Memories and Reflections

Memories of a London Evacuee

The year was 1940 and I was 8 years old. War had been declared the year before, and children in London were told that they would be leaving home to live in the country to avoid the heavy bombing which Germans were inflicting on London.

I was born in 1932 in Woolwich Arsenal, which the Germans were after, being where the guns and shells were made for the defence of this country. My mother worked there during the war. When it came to our turn to go there were over 500 of us children to leave S.E. London.

As far as I can remember we all had our gas masks, a small case and a label on our coats. My cousin was with me, but in the process we got separated and he ended up in Over just outside Cambridge. I remember being put on a train with hundreds of other children somewhere in the City at a main station where we divided into groups onto trains going in different directions. I ended up in a group of a few hundred that ended up in Cambridge. Finally we were sent to Fulbourn, where we were taken to a large building in the centre of the village, and on to a large white cottage down a lane to the left of the building. A Lady whose name I cannot remember showed me where I would sleep, which was a small room at the top, and I remember that I had to go through a small door to get there. It was very strange to me after having a large bedroom at home.

Well, after settling in it was nice to have fresh eggs in the morning for breakfast before going to my first school in the centre of the village not far from the main Church. It was only a small school, but I was not there very long because a lone German plane dropped an unexploded bomb in the front garden of the cottage I was in. It fell during the night and the first I knew of it was when the village policeman and a fireman woke the family up and told us to evacuate the cottage. I can't remember much after that, only that I was taken to another family at either 80 or 82 Pierce Lane where Mr and Mrs Franklin lived with their daughter Rene Parker, whose husband was in the services.

They were very nice people who treated me very well although Mr Franklin had his rules which I had to keep. I was still at this time at the Village school and I used to walk from home to the school and then home again after lessons.

Well, that was the start for me in village life. My family travelled down to see me whenever they could but being war time it was not very often. Next door to where I was staying were Mrs Stanford and two boys, Maurice Still and Owen Hart, and on the other side I believe were the Hawkins family with girls and boys. Maurice, Owen and myself had good times together, whether going down Cow Lane near the Poor's Well where we used to go into the marshy area via a footpath to the left down to a stream, when in the warm weather we used to take our shoes and socks off to paddle as far as we could downstream.

Sunday mornings I was made to go to Sunday School at the church and after a while I joined the church choir, where I stayed until the end of the war. Every Saturday morning and during the school holidays I helped the local milkman Jack White on his rounds with his horse Kate pulling the milk float around. It was good fun helping Jack as I got to know a few of his customers, especially a Mrs Gilbey and her daughter Enid. Mrs Gilbey used to give me a bit of cheese and butter to go with a small round loaf which the local baker used to bake for me to eat on the round, and when Jack got to the pub outside the Fulbourn Station, I either had a lemonade or a glass of milk while he had a drink.

After leaving the village school I had to walk with Owen and Maurice up to the bus stop which was quite a walk to catch the bus to Bottisham College. I enjoyed it there as there was lots to do. The teachers were great too, in particular Mrs Parker and Mr Williams. There were large playing fields where we had football and cricket for the boys, and netball and rounders for the girls. Next to the fields was an airfield which was occupied by the American Air Force. We used to watch them dropping canisters on parachutes and a few times we were caught by the teachers looking out of the windows instead of getting on with our lessons.

I learnt a lot of country life while I was there, collecting corn after the cutters had been round the field, I believe it was called gleaning. We picked blackberries to take home and scrumped for fruit whenever we could, also I learnt a lot about farm life and Jack White asked me if I would like to help on his farm during the holidays after doing the milk round.

When the war ended I was 13 and glad to go home, but I was sad to be leaving all the wonderful friends I had made and the wonderful welcome I had given to me while I was with you all. Once again, thank you all.

Harry West
first printed in The Mill October 2010

Fulbourn Institute Football Club. The seasons 2003 to 2006

Before getting to the seasons 2003 to 2006 it is worth recalling the history of Fulbourn Institute F.C. Founded in 1902, the first real records show that the club was playing from 1921 in Division Two of the County League before being placed in Division 1A when the league was re-organised in 1931-32. Much of the post war era was spent in Division 1A but by the mid sixties the club had made it to the top flight in local football. The greatest achievement came in 1971 when the club took the Premier League title. The Premier League Cup came to Fulbourn in 1983 and 1990. Up to 2003 Fulbourn had always been regarded as a well-respected and well run village football club happily jogging along in the Cambridgeshire League, probably having more downs than ups. Over the years the facilities at the recreation ground improved greatly, providing extra pitches and an improved pavilion.

Things were to change dramatically. Along came the management team of Dave Abbs and Dick Collinge. Both men had a vast experience of football at many levels and had achieved a great deal of success with the clubs they had been associated with. Both men lived in Fulbourn and they couldn't resist the challenge of taking their local team to the highest possible level. A talented team of players was assembled. Many had played their football in the village's successful colts teams. It is worth noting that the success that was to follow would be achieved mostly with players living in the village or the surrounding area. With a combination of first-rate training, clever tactics and a wonderful team spirit on and off the pitch, honours would soon start to arrive.

The major honours in local football are the League Championship, the League Cup and the County Cup. This is known as the treble. No team in local football had ever achieved the treble in one season. Fulbourn Institute did just that in the 2003/2004 season. After this success everyone knew that the 2004/2005 season would be hard. Every team in the county would want to beat them. No team had ever won the treble two seasons running but Fulbourn did it, making local football history once again. It may have looked easy but success was only achieved due to the hard work and commitment of the players and the management team.

The time had come for the club to try and progress to a higher level of football. The success hadn't gone unnoticed and the Cambridgeshire Football Association and the Ridgeons League were very supportive and keen for the club to be playing at a higher level. Although the recreation ground wasn't up to Ridgeons League standard, special dispensation was given for Fulbourn Institute F.C. to play in Division 1 of the Ridgeons League for the 2005/2006 season. Now Fulbourn Institute F.C. was about to play teams from all over East Anglia - Felixstowe, Gt. Yarmouth, Gorleston, Ely, Saffron Walden, Haverhill, Stowmarket, Stanway and many more. What a season it would turn out to be!

The first home game against Gorleston was best summed up by the report in the Cambridge Evening News. 'It was a momentous occasion for the club, and maroon and claret decked the recreation ground as eager villagers (186) turned out to cheer on their team. It was the first time the club had produced a programme, a fact not lost on four fans who made their way to the game from London hoping it would be a collectors item'. Fulbourn won the game 3-1.

The best match I have ever witnessed at the recreation ground was against Stanway Rovers. Both teams were seeking promotion and every point was vital. It was a match that had just about everything. Both teams played wonderful football in front of an enthusiastic crowd of nearly 200. The moment I will never forget came 10 minutes from the end with the score at 0-0. A cross came in, our centre forward just beat the goalkeeper to the cross with his head and the ball started trickling towards the goal line. I am convinced that the spectators behind the goal sucked the ball into the net before erupting, like the rest of the crowd into a frenzy of delight. Fulbourn won 1-0.

After the game, while socialising with the visiting team and officials, the Stanway Chairman remarked what a great match we had witnessed. A credit to football and the League were his feelings. He felt Fulbourn F.C. had put the village on the football map and that everyone must be immensely proud of the club's achievements. The future looked bright for the club, the supporters and the village. It did indeed. The club finished third in the league and would have gained promotion to a higher league. This was another milestone as no new club to the league had ever gained promotion in their first season. History was about to be made again.

To meet ground requirements for the Ridgeons League it was obvious that the recreation ground wasn't fit for purpose, so an alternative site was needed. A piece of land adjacent to the recreation ground was generously offered to the football club by a local landowner. This appeared to be an ideal site for the development of a new ground that would meet the minimum criteria set out to remain in the league. A tremendous amount of hard work by a group of volunteers saw plans drawn up for the new ground. This wasn't a Wembley, an Old Trafford or the Emirates Stadium as rumours in the village suggested, but a fairly modest development. Plans were submitted to South Cambs District Council; they rejected the plans on June 6th 2006.

Although no team had been able to beat or overcome Fulbourn Institute F.C. on their record breaking run, unfortunately individual and collective opposition and lack of support from the Parish Council had beaten the football club's ambitions. The adventure, the dream, was over. Councillor Neil Scarr, who supported the application, said 'Fulbourn Football Club is one of Fulbourn's success stories, no question. If you chuck this out Fulbourn Football Club will not find another site. It will be 20 years of talking to the Parish Council. That's game over.'

Yes, the game was over, no more progression through the leagues, no more making history. Fulbourn were back to the Cambs League and playing village football again. If I go to the recreation ground and see Fulbourn playing my mind wanders back and I think, if only. Albert Wright probably summed up the years 2003 to 2006 best. Albert had played for the village team, with distinction, in the late 1940s and early 50s. When he retired from playing he remained active within the football club and helped on the committee for many years. This was recognized by the Cambridgeshire Football Association, who presented him with a long service award. Albert proudly said " I never thought I would see this at Fulbourn." I knew what he meant, the team playing wonderful football, getting to the Ridgeons League and seeing so many villagers, young and old, getting so much enjoyment out of the experience. I said to Albert "You know we were lucky, we were there, we experienced it and saw what could be achieved. Unfortunately generations to come won't have that pleasure." Sadly Albert agreed with me.

The Sports Development Officer, when supporting the Football Club's application, wrote some profound comments. She said 'After achieving third place this season, they (1st Team) will become local heroes which will bring the community together and encourage youngsters to play, to enable talented players to stay within their local club helping the retention of both club players and coaches at all levels.' What she wanted to happen unfortunately has been lost. The best players, managers and coaches have gone to other clubs and sadly young talented players are looking to progress their careers at other clubs away from the village. This is a great loss to the football club and the village.

The success and achievements of the 2003/2006 season have now been filed in the annals of history. One can only hope that if sometime in the future, if by some miracle it were to happen again, with more support and foresight perhaps Fulbourn Institute F.C. like the Pheonix, might rise again. The years 2003 to 2006 showed that with ambition, enthusiasm and dedication anything is possible, and some fortunate people still have wonderful memories of those years.

Jack Levitt

Nature Reserve

I've made some very good friends on the Nature Reserve...it has enriched my life.

I have learnt to appreciate the changes of season, light, sky; and captured them in photographs, or merely in my imagination.

January morning, and a thick hoar frost. The trees glisten with white gloves on, and the hard knobbly ground withstands a heavy booted footfall. Breath condenses on my scarf pulled high to keep out the icy air. Behind the outstretched fingers of a tree, the white land rises to a colourless sky. Only the few wisps of cloud, blown upward as the ground rises for the first time since Russia, define a horizon - and the pink orange glow, which announces the imminent arrival of the sun. The dog excitedly follows the trail of a rabbit, or stray pheasant, and I watch as a hot, green/gold light grows like a halo round the crown of the tree, its core a white shining circle.

Mid-day in mid summer. I lean on the gate, looking at my favourite oak tree, across an English meadow of buttercups and cow parsley. I can hear bees and other insects, and a slight whispering of a breeze through the long grass and the high leaves in the woods. I wish I could recognise birds by their songs – though the woodpeckers and the Cuckoo are frequent recognisable sounds...A hum of motorway traffic is the only reminder of the era – the view must have been the same on a summer day half a century ago.

It was always our place. Our conversations, our silences – we shared family stories, the meaning of life, my phobia of worms – yours of cows...your adage about 'oak before ash in for a splash, ash before oak, in for a soak' – I'm sure it isn't true, but I think of it every time I pass the oak tree. I sometimes just sit on the log, and remember ...I've been to see where you are in the cemetery, but I couldn't find you – for me you are in the breeze through the leaves, or even the worm at my feet under 'our' tree.

Bluebells in Fulbourn's Nature Reserve

The sun casts dappled shadows on the woodland floor. Beech trees give the best autumnal canopy. The air smells of 'mellow fruitfulness' – ripe apples, just-turned-earth after the harvest, and steam rising out of the hollow ends of straws!

The sun shines from the rising field across to the woods, bright and clear still, though perceptibly lower in the sky as the year turns the globe on its axis. By the time it reaches me it is infused with the copper orange colour of leaves clinging to their branches, waiting for the first heavy winds and rain which will rip them off, to make the carpet which feeds the snowdrops and bluebells. Between the tall straight trunks, the ivy grows in almost solid piles altering the terrain – paths once frequented become overgrown, whilst others, which were mere animal trails only a few years ago, have become wide carriageway avenues.

Because of the hours I have spent walking and thinking, my life has taken turns it wouldn't otherwise have done. I have thought my way out of problems, learnt other ways of seeing the world.

There is an inevitability about one season following another with some subtle changes of vegetation, temperature – or animal tracks and rabbit holes, which helps to give shape to my turbulent and fast-moving year, and a stability to an unstable world. It is clichéd to say the sun rises and falls, and the ground freezes and melts, but it offers a certainty which I depend on – and want to come home to.

I suppose my reason for living in a village is actually to do with what surrounds it!

Helen Kingsley

Fulbourn Flow...

As I sit here, the May morning sun pouring through my box bedroom window, (we're lucky, we have a south facing front garden!) I can see the trees dance to the breeze and spy the view of lush green grass amongst the sporadic hedgerows across the way. I can hear the rush of vehicles pelting down Shelford Road, coupled with the thunderous rumblings of large lorries as they trundle by.

Mixed with the delightful tweeting of birds and shock of traffic that flashes in and out of this idyllic peace, are the sounds of children speaking to their 'grown-ups' and the clip and score of scooter bases and wheels as they make their way to school in the village. My neighbour hangs out her washing; the weather truly is glorious today! The blossom continues to fall gently as our resident birds dart about with what seems like pleasure.

Life as a Fulbourn resident is very pleasant. However I always feel 'new' even though I have lived here for almost 5 years now. I consider myself a foreigner as my origins herald from the North, but I also consider myself in *raptures* with this lovely village of ours.

It has such potential and strength of community. There are always a multitude of 'happenings'...I often tell my friends it's a little like living in an episode of Midsomer Murders or Miss Marple...everything can seem so quaint at times, what with village fetes and jam stalls, local knitting groups and church dinners...!

Fulbourn is obviously not simply a pretty place to be where one can feel incredibly British and twee, it has a wealth of villagers from many, many backgrounds; black, white, Chinese, Turkish, American...and Northern! We appear to have a thriving youth culture some of which is akin to the negative 'hoodie' stereotype seen on TV, but plenty that almost replicates that 'antique' feel...I often see children playing in groups on the greens or streets...I think it's wonderful that they have freedom like this. I suppose it to be similar to the freedom that the children of Fulbourn's past might have had.

My house is modest; my family pretty ordinary; and our daily lives filled with demands and routine. We attempt to 'join' in on this community vibe as much as possible, as much as our children allow, and we like to show our children what an amazing place they live in. From exploring the Nature Reserve, to looking on the Townley Manor, St Vigors church and all our wonderfully convenient shops, our children feel secure in their surroundings and I suppose when one has children, that is an important aspect of life that you wish to give them. Familiarity, accessibility...Fulbourn is almost perfect for bringing up kids. Just another reason why this Northern girl has fallen so deeply in love with it!

I'm not certain what our village anthology will hold within its pages, I could sure write much, much more about the beauty and intricacy, the vibrancy and swell of life here. I always say the only thing is it has no natural waters excepting the dyke, however, it has always had its own 'flow' and rhythm. In short, my hopes for the future of our village are simple...that it continues to bubble away underneath with artistic and community focussed passions, clubs and groups and like Champagne shine and glint with pride as the bubbles appear at the top. It is, after all, the *only* place I've ever seen free roaming chickens on a Wednesday afternoon scratching at the roadside! You see, it fascinates me! It captures me! This village does well with it's wealth of colour, idea, person and variety and my wishes are that it always recognises the diversity within it's very British appearance and continues to grow and maintain this wonderfully calm yet interesting pace of life.

Much like the ever present fields surrounding us, some adorned with golden yellow buds, others full and lush with tall grass, I hope that for me and my family and those of this beautiful village it continues to be so inspiring...and one day we may even become part of its historical tapestry ready to point out to the next generation what they have here and how they can appreciate it.

Jody Palfreyman

On Fulbourn Fen

Where I was born, the white bones of the earth were laid bare. The hills defined the world, and in places the trees and grass gave way to the chalk; a shoulder-blade, a hip, a skull. On the crest of the hills rabbits nibbled the grass as short as moss, and there were views to marvel at. Elsewhere, thick woods clung to the slopes. Their roots made steps, and traps, as you climbed. I remember oak, birch, sweet chestnut, beech. I knew the names of the hills, and I knew the trees as friends.

My children were born only a few miles from here. They find steep hills alarming, almost unnatural. To them all landscapes should be wide, and the sky should reach out, bigger than the world. The top of Fleam Dyke is a splendid height and the open meadow is their special place.

I miss my hills, and the endless woodlands, yet I am learning this place too. The countryside here wears snow more stylishly, the loose hedgerows marking out the perfect whiteness of each huge field. There are more wildflowers here to wonder at, to observe as they change and succeed each other. There is more weather to see and smell, to anticipate or predict, and most certainly less rain to fall. I am learning the names of the meadows and the paths, and befriending the wild sky.

Jackie Duckworth

Fulbourn Fits

It may be hard to see the similarity between Fulbourn and the industrial north of England, but----

I spent my 'formative years' living between Manchester and Rochdale in a 'village' environment. The village ran along the main road, a branch of the canal was close by and the buses ran every 10 minutes. I went to the local Church of England primary school and later to the grammar school in a small town en route to Manchester. (No such thing as Greater Manchester in those days.)

Since then I have spent varying periods of time living and working in Cornwall, Oxford, Sheffield and South Wales. For the past 30 odd years I have lived in Cambridge, the last 14 of them in Fulbourn, and Fulbourn just feels right. From the moment I realized I could afford a new build and watched my house rise from its foundations on the edge of the village I knew I had finally found my comfort zone. Fields to the back that carry on south until you hit Stansted (well it looks that way), a glimpse of the windmill between the houses opposite and those wonderful East Anglian skies and sunsets, constantly changing, always beautiful; a drive each morning over the hill, watching the seasons alter the fields almost daily. Convenient shops, almost all one really needs only a 10-minute walk or quick bike ride away.

If you establish your perfect environment in childhood how does this work?

Squeezed in between Manchester and Rochdale was an area of green belt land. My family were lucky enough to live there - half a mile up an unmade road, a 10-minute walk or a bike ride away from the main road, bus stops and the local small shops run by formidable Lancashire ladies. Fields surrounded our house (the old vicarage) and the primary school (the old church) was next door. The extraordinarily familiar feeling of Fulbourn's old school when it housed the library brought back happy memories. Small farms scattered down and further up the lane were our nearest neighbours. This was my home from the age of

6 until about 19; it formed my ideas of comfort and security. I have found over the years that town living is not for me.

You may fail to see the similarities, after all Lancashire is pretty hilly, but the essentials are there. A vibrant community, local amenities and most importantly for me space, light, green in all imaginable shades and air to breathe freely.
For me, Fulbourn just fits.

Halina Szutowicz

Letter to a friend

My dear friend,

Today I would like to tell you about the village I live in.

When we were moving here I was given warnings about village life: that you might like the closeness and tight-knit relationship between its inhabitants but could easily feel rebuked by this very proximity and watchfulness... but frankly this village has something special because, once visited, it is adopted.

Fulbourn embodies a big, extended family, made of all ages, beliefs, ways of living, wealth, experience, all bonded in one village: you feel close and connected to one another, undoubtedly emotionally related, whilst at the same time still totally unique and different from everyone. As a mother and grand-mother I'm sure you know what I mean about family life and the contradiction of loving them whilst equally sometime wanting time and space from them.

For me Fulbourn is that family, as if my overseas relatives had stepped over the Channel into Cambridgeshire, transported over time and countries, to blossom into this lively place.

And it is here that my fiancé warmed to the idea of marrying me.... How this village turned my quiet husband-to-be into a very relaxed groom, enjoying the whole village crowd around him, will remain something of a miracle, but one thing is sure: this would never have been possible in any other place!

From start to finish and in all aspects, numerous little hands worked humbly towards transforming our dream of "a wedding with a difference" into the reality of a Fulbourn festive and vibrant village celebration, a total community event.

As a true sign of affection for us everyone endeavoured to help shape the day to the couple we are and nothing was "too much". In a number of sensitive touches everyone nurtured and supported our project and played their own part into our innovative wedding fête, from our very young ring-bearer practicing her first steps, to the bell ringers giving their all till the end of the service, or the unique and tailor-made delicate flower arrangements, the surprise balloons and confetti, the last minute amateur photographer coming to the rescue, even the French flags waved in the middle of the church service as we were declared husband and wife at the raising of everyone's glass, and the team helping organise and serve the food and drinks.

The wedding, St Vigor's church

Those involved merged into a united community, bound by a very tangible care and love for each other. My new husband and I were overwhelmed by the obvious desire from all villagers to give the best of themselves for us and we were lavished with presents such as people bringing scrumptious lovingly made and often so professional looking dishes for the "bring and share lunch" in amongst the aisles, following the service. No one will ever forget the sumptuous French wedding cake, a "Pièce Montée" totally created and splendidly made by two ladies of the village! Simply amazing. We all witnessed our village becoming a true community and growing together through each one of us.

We all leave a mark in life, however insignificant it might seem to us, and it is an uplifting thing to keep the memory of the people who lived before us and to carry the baton to later pass it onto the generations to follow. What can we learn or take from other people's lives?

Just as in one big family, Fulbourn displays the rich tapestry of time, from its newborn babies and the young to the mature and old. I enjoy watching the life and choices of all ages, to see what moves them and motivates them in their life decisions.

Dearest friend, I know that you are coming to that stage of your life where you can look a long way back and I feel privileged that you often let me sit with you to turn the pages of life and to tell you of the wonderful moments in my life. I look forward to seeing you again soon.

Véronique Wignall

IMPRESSIONS

(Childhood and Return)

In a way, coming home
Memories abound
Present replaces past
Returning after a lifetime
Expressing joy coupled with uncertainty
Some things so familiar, but most different and unknown
Still doubt lingers over move
In an instant all changes with overwhelming welcome
Over tired with upheaval
Nesting again anew
Settled at last!

I grew up in Fulbourn as a young child during the 1940s. In this beautiful rural village we were cushioned from most of the atrocities of World War II, though I well remember that my mother heard the heavy drone of the German bombers set for Coventry and later saw the sky lit up by the devastation. The war for us was an enchantment with silver paper dropping from the skies like magic, and chocolate from Canadian soldiers camped in the village. Though there was strict food rationing, we did not notice any deprivation, except perhaps the total absence of sweets! The dropping of a VII rocket in an outlying field off the Balsham Road, while being ploughed, was another remembered incident. It thankfully did little damage, but must have surprised the farmer! We were amazed by the massive crater.

Then, far too soon, I was sent away to school; but always able to return in the holidays to the joy of this magical place, with woods, open fields and fens, revealing the wonder of the huge East Anglian skies. I did not fully appreciate, until much later in life, being able to roam free in all this beauty we took for granted, in an age before universal television.. Too quickly I grew up and moved away. In the exuberance of youth, with so much before me, I never thought to return; but return I have, many years later.

Now we are well settled, the return has been a delight, though initially there were misgivings. Converting a building and adding on was a huge challenge, which I like to think the village enjoyed as much as ourselves, being able to view progress with both house and garden through the hedge. We have had a marvellous welcome, made many friends, and take part in activities, which appeal.

Fulbourn is now much larger than the village I remember from childhood. But it still retains the special village feel at its core. Because of its increased size it is now able to offer much more to the residents in the way of shops, services, activities, recreation and just wellbeing. In all it is a perfect place to live.

Selina Sinker

The World is a Village

There are many different nationalities living in Fulbourn, so to illustrate this I interviewed a small sample of my friends, one from each 'corner' of the world. Most of my interviewees arrived here from the other side of the world and settled here to make Fulbourn their home.

Marie-Ann Ha – New Zealand / Southern Hemisphere

Until Marie-Ann Ha arrived in Fulbourn with her family eight years ago, she had spent her life as a 'kiwi nomad'. The hospital in Christchurch, New Zealand in which Marie-Ann was born was destroyed in the 2011 earthquake. Marie-Ann spent her childhood in Christchurch and a very small rural village called Ross, on the West Coast of the South Island. She went to university in Dunedin, and prior to coming to the UK lived in Dunedin, Hamilton and Auckland.

Employment brought Marie-Ann and her husband Tom (originally from Borneo) to the UK, initially to Scotland. They have been married for 20 years and have two children, Imogen aged 12 and Sam aged 16. In 2003, the family arrived in Fulbourn and they live on the Balsham Road, with a menagerie of animals including chickens, two Lassa Apso dogs and four guinea pigs.

"The big differences between Fulbourn and New Zealand," says Marie-Ann "are the friendly community here and the weather." She feels there is a much friendlier community here compared to Auckland, Christchurch, Dunedin and Edinburgh. "Compared to New Zealand, Fulbourn is hotter in summer and cooler in winter. In New Zealand, the summers are longer and the winters are shorter".

"Whilst I miss the wildness of New Zealand, I do appreciate the 'right to roam' we enjoy here in the UK. It is very special to be able to enjoy the beauty of Fulbourn Nature Reserve. I love watching the changing seasons and especially the way the colours change. I love being so close to the rural areas."

The best of times

One of the best qualities of living here in Fulbourn is the community here and the way it cares. "A friend of mine died," says Marie-Ann "and everyone helped, but not in obvious ways. It was lovely for the family. The little things going on in the background really impressed me".

"I have noticed that if you give something to the community, you will receive something in return. I was accepted because I was doing things for the community and other doors have opened since. People see you are committed, getting involved and giving and they respond to it!" says Marie-Ann.

As a Public Health Nutritionalist, Marie-Ann is passionate about growing her own food especially vegetables. She has advised various councils, government and charities about how nutrition affects the population. She has advised council catering services as the law for improving nutritional standards of school meals came into effect.

"Things have really changed here in the last 20 years. The cost of meat here has always been high compared to New Zealand. The quality of food has increased since we arrived. I really enjoy food in season; there is no greater luxury than picking your own fruit for breakfast. I particularly appreciate picking wild blackberries at the Fulbourn Nature Reserve; you just can't pick food in the wilds of New Zealand!"

"I expect I'll be buried here if I have my way!"

Edye Hoffmann – representing USA – Yankee Foodie comes to town!

Edye Hoffmann was born in Colorado but raised in California. She met her future husband Alastair in Utah and they married in Scotland in 2002.

She says they arrived 'by accident' in Fulbourn in 2005, having been gazumped out of two rental places, after Alastair had taken a job down the road at ARM. On their first night they slept on the floor. Waking up the next morning, Edye had expected to see the beautiful historical buildings of Cambridge, and instead was met with a somewhat different view of horses cantering across the flat fens.

When asked what brought her to Fulbourn. Edye says that lots of people were praying that Edye and Alastair would find a place here, and funnily enough the places they looked at outside of the village, just never worked out. She says: "By that time, Fulbourn had sunk its claws into us!"

During their first year in Fulbourn, Edye got involved with Twelve, the church shop in the High Street which now sells fair trade goods and second-hand books. She also volunteered at the Fulbourn Library.

Just one year later, Edye and Alastair bought their first home together in Wrights Grove.

Food exchange builds international relations

Edye recalls one of her best times in Fulbourn "was meeting my first neighbour, an elderly gentleman who was feeding the birds in next door's garden. "He was rather 'shell-shocked' when I spoke to him over the garden fence – because I had actually spoken to him. I took him some 'banana bread' the following week – another look of sheer terror crossed his face". And so began an ongoing food exchange which continues to this day, although they are no longer neighbours. His initial reaction was explained when he confided that he was not actually a fan of Americans. This was as a result of his war time experiences. The American servicemen used to turn up with boxes of oranges and panty-hose to impress the ladies and he just could not compete".

"It has been challenging adapting to the reserve of the English – it took a year for people to reach out to me. Rather than just make polite conversation – I wish there was a guidebook about 'How to cope with the English reserve'."

She continued: "When Americans ask 'Hi – how are you?' They really mean it. There is an expectation that you won't reply with more information than you are really willing to share".

"We take for granted the kind of exchanges we offer to people, that can have a plethora of meanings, the nuances for example – to assume I am right doesn't always help with international relations!"

"Fulbourn is home for me. Whilst I miss my family in the USA, I am not homesick for America," Edye concluded.

Agnes Midgley – Fulbourn's 'ray of sunshine' from the West Indies

Agnes was born in Nevis in the West Indies. It is a small Caribbean island with sandy white beaches and palm trees surrounded by a clear blue sea.

In 1961, at the age of 15, Agnes and her brother arrived in the UK to join her parents, already living in the cold, grey city of Leeds. Her father, a stone mason, passed away just before she arrived in England, so her mother brought her up. Her father had done masonry in some lovely houses in the West Indies.

She had not seen her mother for five years, and in the meantime her Grandma had been looking after her in the West Indies.

"I never knew what it was to be cold until I arrived in England; it was the middle of June. I could not bear being closed in and being inside most of the winter. The first time I saw snow, I said I'm not going out in that!"

However, every cloud has a silver lining. Ten years later she met and married her husband Gordon, as a result of working at the same wholesale chemist in Leeds. They will be celebrating their Ruby Wedding in 2011.

Agnes struggled to settle in Leeds:- "It was just too big for me. I prefer being in a smaller place. You get through it and adapt, but it did take me ages to settle down."

So Gordon and Agnes chose Cambridge and moved to Fulbourn.

Agnes' first impression of Fulbourn was very friendly. "I'm the kind of person who will speak to everybody. At that time it was quite unusual to see a black person in the village. I had no problems whether people would speak to me or not. I used to go up to the village and say 'good morning' and one day they said 'hello, here comes a ray of sunshine – she's always happy."

Gordon worked for 25 years at Marshall Aerospace working in Project Management, involved in the manufacture of aircraft parts, up to retirement eight years ago.

Agnes retired at the same time having worked at Addenbrooke's Hospital for 20 years; she was involved with the employment of consultants.
Agnes and Gordon raised their two boys Neil and Peter in Fulbourn. "It was very easy for them growing up here." Both boys are now in their 30's. Neil works as an Analytical Chemist on the Cambridge Science Park after a number of years in professional sport. Peter is in Lyon, France teaching English to young French professionals having spent some years in London, working in IT after graduation.

The best of times

The best time in Fulbourn has been "Having my two children, being involved in village things – revolving around the school, where our boys played a lot of sport and other activities."

Agnes was also blessed by having good neighbours, when she moved to Fulbourn.
She joined a number of local clubs such as 'Fulbourn Wives' now known as 'Fulbourn Ladies', and made many life long friends.

The worst of times

Agnes has struggled with the cold weather. "I hated being cold and damp, but I had to get used to it. Compared to Leeds, it is much warmer down here. Being born on a small island, I found I was much happier in a small place like Fulbourn, with everybody together."

"Fulbourn is my home. I've lived here for 30 years now and can't think of living anywhere else." Agnes has seen a lot of changes in the village, new houses being built, and the structure of the Centre. There used to be a general store and newsagent run by the Beaumont family (where 'Twelve' is now). There was a petrol station, (where the car salesroom is now), and a wool shop and also a shoe repair shop.

"I go back to the West Indies to visit family but I'm always happy to get back home here."

"I came to England – met my husband and had two boys – added bonuses!"

Véronique Wignall – representing Europe

Véronique Wignall grew up in Lyon, one of the biggest cities in France after Paris. One of four children, her father was a Director of a printing company and her mother, a housewife.

She arrived in the UK in 1993, initially to stay with friends in Essex "for a couple of months". She returned home for a brief spell before starting a teaching job back in the UK. After teacher training at Homerton College, Cambridge, she qualified as a Language teacher. She speaks four languages: French, English, German, Spanish and a little Russian.

"We were looking for somewhere to rent as I was teaching in Cambridgeshire," says
Véronique. "And one day just happened to stop in Fulbourn at Amanda's café for refreshments. It occurred to us that Fulbourn would be a nice village to live in. A few years later, we found a place to rent in Town Close, Fulbourn."

She arrived in Fulbourn in 2006 with her partner Michael.

Lyon can be a very anonymous place. Véronique is very attracted to Fulbourn by the friendliness of people in Fulbourn. When she walks into the village from her house, it is not unusual for her to meet at least three people to stop and have a chat with en route.

Véronique said:
"One of the best days in Fulbourn was the first day we arrived. We had all our boxes at our new rented home, and were unpacking. We needed some refreshment, so we walked into the village, and happened upon the Advent Fair. We met the vicar and curate who welcomed us in. We were amazed to see how friendly people were and how truly interested in who we were. Later that week, two days later someone delivered a Mill (the local magazine) to our new home with a note of welcome!"

The Fulbourn Family
Today, Fulbourn is like a second family to Véronique with all that it entails. i.e. people you feel closer to and people who perhaps you are not so close to. "That's why we got married in Fulbourn in March 2010. The village offers the family I just don't have here in the UK".

“I really care for the people in Fulbourn because I know they really care for me – like a big family. I feel I’m really lucky to have a variety of people and the bonds I have with them.

“What we’ve got is very precious here. Let’s nurture it and learn to accept each other and live (harmoniously) together. A low point for Véronique is when she hears people gossiping, as she feels it can damage what we have here. “It hurts each other.”

“I feel people have accepted me as I am. Whilst I’m regarded as French, I don’t feel an outsider.”

“If you are a globetrotter, you never know quite where you will end up – home is where you make it!” Véronique concluded.

Gill Godber

Moving To Fulbourn

People move to Fulbourn for many different reasons; some to find work, some because of work, and some to retire, or to be nearer family or friends; others, just to be able to join in village life. Many are just returning to their roots. I am sure that there are other reasons too but this is our story.

We moved to Fulbourn in the summer of 1988. It was at the time when house prices were going up at a tremendous rate each month in the area but well before the prices had started to rise in South Yorkshire. South Yorkshire in the 1980's suffered from a very high unemployment rate due to the closing of the mines and the steel works by the Thatcher government. Work or promotion was hard to come by so we decided it was time for us to move on. We could have moved to Scotland, Bristol or Cambridge; John was offered the job in Cambridge so we moved south.

John moved in 1987 and rented a room in Romsey. I continued to work in Sheffield waiting for a transfer with the Civil Service. Whenever John had free time he would visit the estate agents and pick out property that he thought we would like or that we could afford to buy. By the time I was able to come down to Cambridge to view the properties they were sold or offers we made were being gazumped. Eventually while visiting a friend in Cambridge we noticed a house in the village. My friend had an idea where it was so we arranged a viewing for the following day. It wasn't quite what we had wanted but by that time we were running out of options so we put in an offer, which was eventually accepted. In the August of '88 we moved in to Number 8. We did plan to move again before long but we never got round to it.

At that time we were both working full time, and had a lot of family commitments in Yorkshire, so for the first year or so we got to know most of our immediate neighbours but not many of the village people. Because of work commitments, John worked shifts and I worked in Ely, most of our shopping was done at Sainsburys so we rarely used the village shops. This all changed when I began to work on the Fulbourn hospital site and we got a new dog.

We began to use the village shops on a regular basis and walking with the dog we got to meet more people. We got to know the nice areas to walk, the nature reserve, the Roman road, and Wandlebury amongst many others. Then in the early 90s I began to work part time so I was able to become more involved in village life. I helped for a number of years at the church fete; I went to coffee mornings to either support or help and gradually became involved with village activities. For a number of years I did house to house collections for a number of charities and made a lot more contacts. When people with children move to a new area they often find new friends meeting at the school gates, taking the children to clubs and activities, for them perhaps it is easier to make contact with like minded people. It's slightly different when you are older.

As time moved on and I retired the newly formed Volunteer Library was looking for extra volunteers. It was time I put something back into my community on a regular basis so I became a volunteer. Once more it helped us to meet more and more people and make lots more friends. As the years have gone by we got to know so many people, not always by name but there is always a friendly face and chance to pass the time of day wherever we are in the village.

So my advice to anybody moving to Fulbourn: there's lots going on in the village, use the village shops, meet people in the high street and get involved in any of the village clubs groups and activities. There's always something going on in Fulbourn.

Ann Sowden

Fulbourn Post Office - a sad demise

I'll just pop down to the Post Office
And buy a stamp or two,
I'll just pop down to the Post Office
My car tax to renew.

I'll just pop down to the Post Office
And get this parcel weighed,
I'll just pop down to the Post Office
And buy a card for Jade.

I'll just pop down to the Post Office
To buy some euros for Eire,
I'll just pop down to the Post Office
To post a letter to Sara.

I'll just pop down to the Post Office
Oh, it's gone!

Jill Woolley

The Village Post Office

Heavy drops of rain fell slowly from the porch entrance to the Post Office. The doors remained firmly shut and no amount of pushing or tugging would open them.

Mrs. Eunice Witherspoon wore a bewildered look. Her mouth, her eyes – her entire face – were contorted into a shape which, in any language, spelled disbelief. Her neighbour from Number 10 happened to pass by.

"Hey, Mrs. Morgan," she cried, "what's up here? It's three o'clock and it's shut."

"It closed almost a week ago, Eunice," she replied, her tone sympathetic.
"Look through the window," she continued, "the shelves are bare. The postmaster has retired and sold the shop And it's not re-opening. Not unless someone takes it over."

"But me pension," grumbled Eunice. "What am I to do? I needs me pension. I've to buy food and I've bills to pay. You know, the 'lectric and the gas. And I need a stamp to post a birthday card."

"Ah, well, the stamp you can get from the Co-op" said Mrs. Morgan helpfully.

"But I only want one and they sell 'em in those books. I just want one."

"Then you'll have to go to another Post Office for everything. There's one in Cherry Hinton. Probably."

Mrs. Witherspoon frowned. "And what a journey that is! Over an hour there and back. And it's so cold today what with me legs an' all."
And then, "What d'you mean – probably?"

“Well, there are so many Post Offices closing … and staying closed. Here today. Gone tomorrow. Our lives are changing. We all need to be on the Net these days.”

“On the *what*?” barked Mrs. Witherspoon.

“The Net … the Internet. We’ve all got to be connected,” replied her neighbour.

“Well, nobody’s connecting me to anything! I’m free to go where I want.” She glanced across the road to the bus stop. “Except for now. I suppose I’d better join the queue. I just ‘ope the windows are clean so’s I can see where my stop is.”

“Goodbye, Eunice – and good luck with the stamp.” She smiled roguishly. “See you on Facebook?”

Mrs. Witherspoon’s head snapped up and it’s as well she didn’t topple over in front of the car speeding out of Manor Walk.

Terry Braverman

Fulbourn's Swifts

In May two hundred years ago and more
in Selbourne, Gilbert White waited, watching
for his swifts to come, black sickles,
sky-riding, wings flickering against the blue.

In Fulbourn, now, we wait watching for them.
Will they accept the mod con new homes
we give them, will they come to the broadcast
calls we send them, will they scream in their
party circling of St Vigor's tower?

Richard Howlett-Jones

(swift logo by Andrew Tanser)

Note: Fulbourn's swifts nested in the old concrete houses of the Windmill Estate. In 2009, there were 72 pairs – the biggest colony in Cambridgeshire. Concern that they would be lost in the rebuilding led to some experimental nests being created in the new house roofspace. In 2010 59 pairs were counted, with 10 using the new nests. A 2011 survey is about to be done.

Hopes and Fears For The Future

How Fulbourn Might Look in the Future

The year is 2030 in high springtime and Fulbourn still exists as a village separate from Cambridge, a village set among trees. The trees are in full leaf and bright green. As seen from the high ground on the Shelford Road the built-up area is contained within a green matrix, though fore-shortened by the distant aspect so that it seems more compact than it actually is. The Green Belt around the village has maintained its integrity despite the building on the old Ida Darwin Hospital site to the west of the village proper.

The vision of the 2009 Parish Plan has been retained and developed. Within the village, wherever the opportunity has occurred, new tree planting has taken place, mainly trees that have a productive function. So fruit and nut trees now adorn some of the awkward corner spaces which were previously just open grassed areas. Particular species include Apple, Plum, Walnut and Sweet Chestnut. The blossom on these trees in the spring gives the village a special feel such that it is now widely known as the Orchard Village.

The old estate orchard in the Nature Reserve is now a favourite place for young people and families to visit and to gather fruit and nuts in season. Coppicing of the hazel and other nut bushes has become a regular interest of residents. The orchard is also popular for picnics. Other small orchards have been planted elsewhere where opportunities occur and new allotments have been provided to meet the ever increasing demand by residents for land to grow vegetables.

All over the village wherever public space permits there are raised beds of herbs, vegetables and summer fruits for people to pick and use as they wish. ' Incredible, edible Fulbourn', following on from the original project in Todmorden in Yorkshire, is now a byword in the locality which sums up the developing resilience of the village community.

The interest in home baking has been spurred on by the repair of the Windmill which now grinds locally grown corn to meet the burgeoning market for locally produced stone ground flour. Not only does the Mill provide for the needs of villagers but it also has a strong following from the surrounding villages and Cambridge itself.

Across the fields, high up by the Shelford Road, the two village wind turbines provide a foil for the original windmill and also power most of the village's electricity needs. The controversy over placing the turbines has died down now most people are pleased their energy costs are so low.

The approach roads give the aspect of broad avenues with the trees planted in the twenty-teens becoming more mature. Traffic, once at a high level, has reduced due to the cost of fuel and most cars and vehicles are powered by electric motors making a sharp reduction in exhaust and noise pollution. Helpfully the Parish Council have provided re-charging points at the Recreation Ground and at one or two other locations. Throughout the village there is a 20 mph speed limit for safety reasons and it is much more pleasant to ride bicycles on the main highways. New routes have been provided for recreational cycling and walking as most residents now spend longer in and around the village in their spare time, enabling them to take advantage of the accessible local countryside.

Residents can now make use of the 'Living Landscape' to the east of Cambridge joining up Wandlebury and the Cherry Hinton Chalk Pits with Fulbourn Fen Nature Reserve and Wilbraham Fen via the Roman Road and Fleam Dyke. This linear 'park' complements other initiatives around the city of Cambridge such as the extension of Wicken Fen to Quy and the new open areas linked to the River Cam to the south and west of the city.

With the completion of the Young People's Centre, housing both the youth club and the scouts, Fulbourn Centre and the Recreational Ground have continued to set a standard of provision for sports, arts and community activities not surpassed in the locality. The large community hall, now extended so a wider range of sports activities can take place, provides a unique venue for major events as well as supplying the community's needs for indoor sport and recreation. The annual arts programme has developed a reputation that extends beyond the local area.

The re-development of the Ida Darwin Hospital site has not had such a deleterious effect on the landscape as originally feared. Tree planting around its perimeter has softened the impact and, with a lower profile to the buildings and the open area between the site and Capital Park, it has been largely absorbed into the landscape.

The electrified bus service to Cambridge and other local centres is much improved and connects with the regular tram service using the railway line. New stations have been built at Station Road, Capital Park. Teversham Road and Cherry Hinton, providing a direct link with the guided busway and mainline rail services at Cambridge Station.

The farmed countryside presents a changing aspect with more hedges and small groups of trees providing interest and also 'green routes' for wildlife to move between habitats. This ensures a better balance between nature and agriculture. The species of trees that have been planted generally take account of the higher temperatures and even drier climate. These include Alder, Downey Oak, Willow, Pine, Lime and Bamboo.

With less use of pesticides and a greater interest in organic methods of farming, together with growing a wider range of crops to meet changing needs, inevitably the landscape has begun to change markedly. Hemp is now a valued crop for sustainable building as well as the harvesting of straw for its insulation properties. The sight of Suffolk Punch horses working the land has also begun to transform the look of the countryside as the reduced use of diesel-powered tractors became necessary in the 2020s due to high fuel costs and the European Common Agricultural Policy.

The High Street continues to provide for the day to day shopping needs of the village and this has been greatly enhanced with the closure of large local supermarkets due to lack of patronage by car shoppers and the impact of internet shopping. Weekly markets are held which allow residents to buy and sell local produce.

With the high costs of travel more people live and work in the village mainly from home, taking advantage of the high speed internet and other communications media. The loss of jobs from the closure of major retails outlets has enabled people to find other employment opportunities serving the social and environmental needs of the community. Expansion of the Day Centre took place to meet the increased needs of the growing aged population living longer, and now there are several services provided. The new Health Centre and Cottage Hospital sited on the edge of the village provides for most of the health needs of the village.

Fulbourn has become a truly sustainable and self reliant community and looks forward to further new initiatives outlined in the new Parish Plan.

Richard Townley

Hateful/Happy Houses

Hateful, horrible houses
Blocking out the sky.
They've filled the empty spaces
And make me want to cry.

When we came to Fulbourn
In nineteen sixty three
The space next door was empty
A green field, without a tree.

When they started 'Jerusalem'
We could not believe our eyes,
The promise it would remain a field
Was just the builders' lies.

But we grew used to our neighbours
The trees began to grow,
Our children playing hide and seek in
Secret places we did not know.

Now there are multicoloured houses
With roofs all pointy and tall
Replicas of Cambourne and Arbury
Which don't suit Fulbourn at all.

In a few years they'll have mellowed
And people will forget
But we wont see the sky from our window
Which will cause us some regret.

So we put up with the noise and dust
While the old is swept away
The homes will block our view of the trees
And a new generation will play.

We hope they'll be Happy Houses
New homes for those displaced
We wish the people in them well
Though they take away our space.

Jill Woolley

The mystery of St Vigor's church clock

Very few people realised that the Clock Winder had retired. Indeed very few people knew that such a person existed. Each week for over 50 years he had walked or cycled to St Vigor's Church, climbed the tight winding stairs to the top of the church tower and carefully wound the clock and the chime. But now he had retired and there was no one to take his place.

It took three days for the hands of the clock to finally stutter and grind to a halt. Then the delicate chime mechanism fell silent and the hourly *dong* announcing the time of day ceased. The absence of a sound goes relatively unnoticed unlike the sudden interjection of a new noise.

The event coincided with the annual return of the swifts to Fulbourn. Every year the birds migrate back from Africa to exactly the same roosting crannies or to new nest boxes cleverly designed during the construction of a new housing complex. The first arrivals were the oldest pair and after briefly filling their untouched crevice with tiny soft material they swept into the sky to feed and replenish their strength. By the third day a flock of seventy birds had arrived and erupted in a cascade of darting wings to celebrate their safe return.

Then the oldest pair swung away from the main flock and circled the church tower. Round and round they hurtled for something was amiss. Something that was part of their homecoming was gone. The tone of their birdsong subtly changed and the movement of their wings indicated an alert. After a few minutes they ceased the spiral and changed course heading for the Fen Nature Reserve.

The four great oaks in the large field witnessed their return and the tiniest rustle in the top branches seemed to reflect their delight. The flock encircled the largest tree and the oldest pair repeated their swirling tight flight like one of Saturn's Rings. The oak's sensitive nervous system picked up the agitation and sucked back the moisture to one small old twig at the top of its canopy. The sudden loss of moisture caused the twig to murmur a soft crack.

A pair of collared doves became nervous by the excited cacophony of swifts that were now a blur of frenzied swirling movement like a high speed revolving umbrella hovering over the tree. Then as suddenly as they had arrived the swifts were gone. The nervous doves trembled on a lower branch and with the departure of the maelstrom fluttered up to perch on the weakened twig, which immediately gave way with a second crack and the poor birds fluttered to recover their composure. The twig plunged down and landed at the base of the oak. The male dove cooed to its mate, spotted the fallen twig and swooped down to pick it up.

*****

Letter to his Grace the Bishop of Ely from the Rector of St Vigor's Church

My Lord Bishop,

I thought it appropriate to write to you regarding the recent strange events surrounding our church clock. You may have seen me interviewed on the local Cambridge BBC TV News followed by numerous articles in the media. For the record this is what happened at my first Evensong Service last Sunday following my new appointment to this Parish.

At the very beginning of Evensong, as I was reading the opening prayer, the church clock began to chime. As it continued I remembered that before my arrival the Clock Winder had retired and no one had taken his place. Momentarily I half expected the clock to chime six but after it continued on I realised something was amiss.

The Churchwarden standing next to me whispered that what was happening was very strange, as the clock had stopped working three weeks ago. Even stranger, the clock was continuing to chime beyond twelve. On and on it chimed and by now the congregation was completely absorbed by the bell and I was compelled to bring the service to a temporary close.

I decided to go outside to look at the clock. I tried to calm everyone down with a quick prayer and then proceeded outside. The clock hands were set on six and the chimes continued relentlessly like a bell calling people to a service.

Yet there was something equally odd. A great mass of swifts was encircling the top of the church tower zooming round and round. Everyone was very disturbed and one man who had witnessed the return of the swifts every year since boyhood commented that the swift's behaviour was unique. Indeed half a dozen parishioners took out their mobile phones and proceeded to photograph or video the scene.

I decided to climb the stairs of the tower to inspect the clock's inside mechanism. The key to the tower door was part of my set of keys. The Churchwarden and the man who knew about the swifts accompanied me. As I moved into the small chamber I heard both the chime of the clock and a soft cooing of doves outside. My colleague, a very sensible and practical man asked how it was possible for the clock and chime to work when the clock had not been wound for so long. The only sets of keys were normally locked in the vicarage safe.

Then I noticed that at the very bottom of a wheel that operated the clock was a small twig jammed into the mechanism. I carefully moved closer and gently glided the twig away. At that moment the clock chime ceased. My companion was incredulous as to how the twig could have got there. The outside of the tower had been recently insulated against jackdaws and he could not see how anything could get in. There was no way in. The sound of the doves grew louder.

We descended the stairs and relocked the entrance door. I could see everyone was still very worked up by the mystery and I decided to calm people down by giving an excuse that a bird had somehow got into the tower and accidently jammed a twig into the clock. People were quick to accept this was the answer and we returned inside to complete Evensong. I subsequently double-checked the clock tower and I still cannot understand how any bird or animal could have got in. How had the clock restarted?

There is one other mystery. The group of people who photographed the flock of swifts flying around the tower have been to see me to say that only a single pair of birds was recorded!

This is extremely strange and no one could offer any suggestion to how six mobile phone cameras could all have malfunctioned in such a manner.

However as a result of all the national publicity a recently retired brother and sister have volunteered to become the new Clock Winders. The clock has been restarted and chimes on the hour. In truth I cannot understand what happened but God works in mysterious ways.

Yours in Christ

PS. I have received a very interesting letter from a Spanish monk called Brother Sebastian. He has a very special devotion to St. Vigor and would like to visit our church because of its rarity and as part of a retreat holiday. I have of course responded positively. His favourite hobby is ornithology and I have promised to show him the famous Fulbourn swifts.

*****

The two elderly swifts produced three young fledglings of which two survived. As summer closed the four birds circled Fulbourn and the parents screeched out a farewell. Soon the rest of the flock joined them and they pirouetted into the sky and began the arduous migration back to Africa.

Using thermals and wind currents they flew south over the sea and then onto the continent of Europe. As it was their first migration, the two youngsters were constantly supported by their experienced parents and other mature birds. The sky is the real home of swifts and it is in the sky where they feed, sleep, and after reaching four years of age they mate in flight.

On and on the flock journeyed, combining various methods and instincts to find their way. They include knowledge of the stars and a strong sense of the north and south poles. The electro currents running around the globe and key landmarks such as mountains, oceans and rivers also provide markers. Winds and currents carry them part of the way but these can also act as a barrier if they drag them off course.

Despite their deep knowledge of the route the two elderly birds slowly felt the wear and tear of the long flight and the buffeting of winds began to take its toll. They rested whenever possible on currents and other adult birds recognised their weakness and fluttered around them in support.

A deep instinct to help their young complete their first migration propelled them on but age was sapping their strength away. Somehow they struggled on as far as Spain and then the male bird felt a spasm and its tiny heart gave out. It dropped slowly down followed by its lifelong mate desperate to stay with him. As he was about to crash to earth her fragile heart shuddered and she died a second before they both tumbled onto the courtyard of an ancient monastery.

Brother Sebastian moved from the cool shade of the cloister to drink a cup of cold water from the fountain in the centre of the square. It was then that he saw the tiny-feathered bodies on two sides of the fountain. With the utmost tenderness he gently picked up the two swifts in both hands and felt their incredible lightness.

He carried the precious couple into a small garden filled with roses and honeysuckle and carved out a tiny grave, covered the spot with soil and placed a few red rose petals on the earth. He crossed himself and then responded to the Compline bell for evening prayers.

Instinctively covering his head with his hood he moved quietly to the monastery chapel and knelt in a honey coloured oaken pew. The silence was palpable and the smell of incense and recently lighted candles pervaded the ancient stone building.

He waited a moment to collect his thoughts and then said a prayer to St Vigor thanking him for the opportunity to bury God's creatures in a dignified way and expressing wonder at the glory of birds in the air. Perhaps only angels could experience such a magnificent place to live.

Then the bell struck again and the ancient prayers of worship began.

David Horace Dobson

....

Footnote

I wrote this story for the Writing Group before I started my research for the historical article on the St Vigor's Church Clock & the Clock Winder. It is dedicated to my two great nieces, Alice and Eve.

I have taken a certain poetic licence regarding the relationship between parent swifts and their offspring. In reality as soon as swift fledglings have hatched they almost immediately leave the nest and become independent. They do not need their parents to guide their migration and they usually fly off before the older birds. However swifts mate for life and can live for as long as thirty years.

The final prefab – The final brick

(destruction of the prefabricated homes behind Cambridge Road, Fulbourn)

The sun's laughing at me today.
Looking down at me – all tears and gloom –
Then moves aside to give me room - then
Looks again but doesn't wonder
Why it is I'm rain and thunder.

I am the final brick that built a house that made a home
And now I lie here, left alone
Whilst all about new buildings rise
Upon the ruins.

A hundred eyes look down upon
My tiny, tiny space – soon gone –
A tiny, dirty brick of clay – and even this they'll take away,
And throw away and toss astray
With careless hands that never felt
The pride with which my walls, once built,
Became a house that made a home.
The final brick now lies alone.

A house no longer, nor a wall,
A brick the sun now laughs upon
A nod, a smile, then hurries on
To greet the future steeply rising
Concrete, turning, churning, sizing
Rows and rows of shiny bricks
And men with forms, and nods, and ticks
To say "well done!" and "weren't we quick?"
And here I am.
The final brick.

Terry Braverman

What life in Fulbourn could be like in 2030

All villages change and evolve and now in 2030, due largely to the high cost of fuel and the need to preserve it, Fulbourn has become largely self-sufficient in food. No longer is most of our food imported and processed in factories but grown locally. Things like tea, coffee, chocolate, bananas and oranges are still imported – what would we do without chocolate? In general we now lead active lives and are healthier and fitter. Facilities in the village have improved to meet the needs of the community and recycling now concentrates on repair and re-use, providing local jobs and helping the local economy. The bird song seems louder as the amount of traffic has reduced and slowed down. And a community bakery has become an important focus for the village.

The general appearance of the village is enhanced by the number of fruit and nut trees that have been planted over the years, and the mixed herb, vegetable and spring flower beds that have sprung up give everyone access to fresh fruit and vegetables and an involvement in their cultivation. The huge amount of knowledge in the village of how to produce good crops and look after the soil gets shared through informal discussions and hands on training. Saving and sharing seeds is well established and ways to share surpluses are well organised. With so much general interest, gardens have become highly productive. Growing food is now very much part of the school curriculum. The library has a special collection of gardening books for anyone to use.

The amount of food that can be produced in gardens, allotments and land-share schemes can be greater than that produced on a large scale because individuals can be more aware and give the plots more attention. And although some crops are better than others there is no longer so much waste because misshapen vegetables taste just as good and they do not have to fit neatly into boxes for long distance transportation.

Another initiative that has become popular is community supported agriculture where members of the community buy 'shares' from local farmers and in return get a weekly box of fruit and vegetables, or they can 'purchase' shares in return for time spent helping the farmer. Thus the farmer has a guaranteed market for his produce and some help with growing it. Also particularly suitable in this area, is growing a variety of cereal crops to make flour now the windmill is working again.

Fulbourn's Windmill, 2011

Above all our food is fresh and tastes wonderful.

Now that processed food has become so expensive due to the cost of running factories and transportation, there is a greater interest in home cooking. People now share recipes and every year the best are put on the village cookery website. The schools have taken this on board and all children leave Primary School being able to cook a basic meal from scratch. The Village College provides more detailed education on nutrition, a wide range of cooking and food preservation skills.

With the need to make the best use of our food people have learned to share ways of preserving surpluses. Fruit like plums, apples and figs are dried in community fruit driers and cider and juice is made using the community fruit press. Traditional ways of storing apples and vegetables for the winter are also much used. A weekly Farmers' Market is held in the High Street where people can buy and exchange local produce.

The community bakery is now well established and the smell of freshly baked bread wafts around the village. The bakery is run as a co-op owned by the community. Using local varieties of flour and with an artisan baker in charge, helped by trained local people, a wide range of breads and other baked goods are produced. The bakery also has a café, and in the corner a Post Office, so that the building has become a real centre of the community and a general meeting place, a place to share information and exchange ideas, recipes and gardening advice. The wealth of knowledge and skills is passed down from one generation to the next.

Slimming clubs are a thing of the past as people take more exercise and eat a better diet, no longer relying on heavily processed food and take-aways. People are fitter and healthier due to growing and eating their own food and using more energy walking, cycling and gardening. With fast efficient public transport it is no longer worthwhile driving into Cambridge and with the internet things not available locally can be ordered on-line and delivered.

Recycling has taken on a new meaning. Where in the past anything that stopped working was put in the bin for recycling or to go to landfill, now there is no more built-in obsolescence. Things are made to last because no one wants to throw away valuable raw materials, and if they do break down, it is more economic to repair them. Fulbourn has a variety of workshops where things can be taken to be repaired or refurbished. Unwanted furniture and household items can be swapped or sold from a local barn so nothing is wasted, and people do not have to spend a lot of money when they need something. With many talented people who can sew in the village, clothes can be easily altered and repaired, or exchanged at regular 'clothes swaps'. All this provides local jobs and practical training.

The need to be more focussed on the village for day to day needs has brought the community closer together and more self-sufficient, making for a friendly and inclusive local society.

Judith Townley

Look after me

Don't feed me rubbish

Don't punch me like a punch bag

Look after me like you do your body

Take care of me like you should

Don't destroy me

Don't walk away – look after me

Don't give to just one, give to everyone

Do stand with me like you stood with your Mum

When you were a child.

Do be by my side when I need your help

Do look after me in every way.

Please!

Georgia Fordham

I wish the world would understand the damage they are doing
That neighbours would treat each other's gardens with respect, and not litter
That I could show the children the rec* with its fresh green grass and the shiny play equipment

I wish the world would understand what they are doing
That they could see what Fulbourn used to look like
That people would use electric cars instead of gas-guzzlers
That I could turn the clocks back and pick up all the litter I dropped in the past

I wish the world would understand the damage they are doing
That I could have shopped at the local stores instead of going to Tesco
That I had caught the bus more often than driving
That I had planted trees to help the forests grow

I wish the world would understand the damage they are doing.

Ellie Scotcher

**rec – the Village Recreation Area*

If I could I would turn back the clock, pick up the rubbish I saw, not add more

If I could I would worship every drop of water I had, not waste it

So here I sit, seventy-six years old

My eyes closed tight

I see the village sleeping gently

The long queues in the Post Office chattering

And children buying one penny sweets

The rec, with families having delicious picnics on the grass

That is what Fulbourn is meant to be.

I open my eyes and there I see the village as it is today

No gas-guzzling cars polluting the main street

Just families riding by on their bicycles

The windmill is waving his hands in celebration

The sun sits in a bright blue sky

The fields are long and wide, waving their crops

The church stands tall and proud

And the local shops are in the heart of the village

I'm so proud I was a part of this.

I sigh with relief

What a wonderful village Fulbourn is!

James Taylor

I wish there were still the greens and orchards I used to play in when I was little
I pray every night that I will wake up from this nightmare -
But I am awake!
If I could I would swim in the lake that used to be behind my house, just one more time
If only my grandchildren could see what it was like when I was young
I wish everyone would understand what they're doing to our world
If only every bad move I made would undo and rewind
Then I would never make that move again.

Olivia Jones

Dirty rubbish set on the ground

I, the village, in the town

I want my city to be safe and sound

Seventy years ago it was fabulous

Now it's a rubbish tip,

Filled with litter on the road

The park that was so beautiful is now smelly and old

So sad, so angry!

I want the water to be clear and sparkly

I want the trees to be green and healthy

I want the flowers to be blooming, laughing

I want happiness, not darkness, not sadness

Olivia Speechley

I am the village. Look after me.
Don't chop down the trees
They are part of me.
Don't flood me with rubbish
Drop it in the bin.
I am the village. Look after me.

I'll deliver all I can
I'll try my hardest
If we all do the right thing
We'll both be fine,
You and me
I am the village. Look after me.

The shops are my heart
Please don't break them
Don't do the wrong thing
Please do the right thing
Or we won't survive.

Tom Campbell

Don't hurt me

By dropping your rubbish all over me

By speeding through my roads

Look after me

Don't hurt me

By turning your back on my shops

By ripping out my heart

Look after me

Don't hurt me

By destroying my trees

By ignoring my tears

Look after me

I belong to you!

Emma Ison

I'm full of regrets

I wish I hadn't been so lazy

I wish I had stopped them building factories

They churn out filthy black smoke which pollutes the air

I wish I hadn't let them litter the streets

Treating the pavements like dustbins

I wish I had stopped them making wider roads for all the traffic

Pushing people off the footpath

I wish I hadn't agreed for them

To destroy the rec and the adventurous nature reserve

I'm full of regrets

I wish I had taken some action.

Anna Loughlan

I am the village, look after me!

That's how it should be.

Please don't feed me rubbish or

I will die.

When you closed the Post Office you

Ripped out my heart

Why are you treating me like this?

But suddenly you have started to put

All the rubbish in the bin where it belongs.

And you are trying to get planning permission

To build a new Post Office

When you polluted the stream it burned my mouth

When you sliced down my trees I struggled to breathe.

Jack Brand

I've given you all my precious resources and what do you give me back?

I know you need me to survive so why do you tire me so?

You're destroying what keeps you alive!

I wish I could be full of bright lights, not drowned in darkness

Why do you feed me with all your waste when

All you're doing is feeding yourself with sadness?

I remember when I used to be a playground all the time

With the sun shining down on your heads

Children would run in my blossoming woods and lie sunbathing in my fields

Now it's gone, gone for good, or that's what you think

But I think it can change!

Esther Tun

I am the village, look after me
I need to sleep and breathe
Don’t feed me rubbish or cut down my trees
We need each other

I am the village, take care of me
Don’t feed me junk
We need each other

I am the village, don’t destroy me
Let me rest and feel refreshed

I am the village, don’t hurt me
Visit my shops and pubs on a winter’s evening and a summer’s morn
Visit my fields, but don’t spoil me
We need each other.

William Hardy

Thank you for looking after me and treating me well
The shops of Fulbourn are my heart
Without them I am not a village.
The seas of grass are remarkable.
Thank you for preserving the woods and the wildlife living there
Thank you for keeping the air fresh by not building factories that
Puff out dull grey smoke from the chimneys.
It raises my spirits to see children having fun playing football down the rec
I am overjoyed that you have not destroyed the rec and built on it.

Matthew Hall

Don’t feed me litter that you leave on the streets, it makes me feel old and unloved

Don’t get rid of the trees

Don’t get rid of the shops: these are my heart so don’t rip it out

The nature reserve is a beautiful sanctuary

It gives the natural world a place to make their home

Thank you for the windmill

I’m quite excited at what’s to come

I believe the school children of this generation will be a gift to me

But just one thing:

I’m your home town so show some

Respect!

Adam Towers

I hope I'm going to be looked after in the future
I pray people will realise I'm not just a dustbin, that I actually mean something
I hope every flower in every garden will be looked after
I hope people won't drive around in big cars when they only drive for five minutes
I hope I'm noticed by someone
I pray people will keep me healthy and look after their surroundings
I hope people realise that I'm home to millions
I hope someone will turn off lights when they're not using the room
I hope people will understand that I'm not an object, that I'm the reason they are alive
I pray my heart will be safe
I hope people recycle their junk and that they don't litter
I pray people will understand that I look after them but they don't look after me
I hope I'm being noticed throughout the world
I wish for a better world in the future
I hope people will ride their bikes more than they drive their cars
I hope people will respect the trees and flowers like they respect people
I pray that there will be just enough rain and just enough sun
I hope people realise that the world won't be here if you don't act
I pray that someone is out working day by day trying to make our world safe and happy

I hope people want their world to be safe
I hope someone will send the message round that our world will change so drastically if we don't help
I hope people will walk more than drive
I hope people will show how much they love their community
I pray people will realise there's a world out there and that it needs looking after
I hope people will use their world to have fun and socialise
I hope people want a world that's a community and not just a place to stay
I dream the world will be safe.

Hannah Lagnado

I am the village
I am where you live
I am all you've got
Look after me
Don't spoil me with rubbish or cut down my trees
The trees are your life's breath
Please leave them alone
I am the village

I am the village
I am all that you've got
I'll provide all I can.
What about you?
I'll battle through storms and work with nature
I'll bring joy to you, my residents
I am the village

The shops are my heart
Don't rip them out
Take care of me
I want to live longer
Keep me healthy
Take time to look after me
I am the village

I look after you with all my might
I depend on you like you depend on me
I'll let you go now and for my sake please remember
I am the village.

Ben Claydon

Look after me!

Stop feeding me disgusting rubbish

Stop choking me with filthy fumes

Stop knocking down trees

Or my heart will soon stop beating

Help me!

Don't ignore me: listen!

Don't hurt me: show me respect!

Don't make me gulp fumes or

My heart will soon stop beating

Listen to me!

I want to hear the birds sing

I want to feel rabbits hopping into the woods

I want to see the sunshine every morning

So my heart beats strongly

Care for me!

Treat me like family; make me feel loved

Don't damage me, admire me

I want everything to be perfect

So my heart will remain beating.

Abbie Lawler

It's now 2075 and I'm proud of my village
I remember when I campaigned for our reliable wind turbines
I remember when I helped save our giant windmill
I remember when I planted some trees in our new wood for you to explore and play in
I was only meant to plant ten trees but Len gave me an extra seed
I remember when me and my chums managed to get the Post Office back
I remember when I got my first allotment, I was so excited!
I remember when I got up at 6 in the morning to get my tools ready
And now, 2075, it's your job to carry on and make yourself proud of your village.

Jazim Ali

I hated it when you ruined the muga*
I hated it when you destroyed the woods
I hated it when you built so many constructions on me
I hated it when you splattered litter on me
I hated it when you destroyed the wildlife
I hated it when you broke down the shops and built a factory which filled the village with black, dirty smoke

I'm so proud of you now
I love it now you are creating more fields and growing crops
I love it now you are making new woodland
I love it now you got rid of the factory
I love it now you're litter picking
I love it now you're being more eco friendly

I gave you me and you gave me care.

Conor Duffy

**muga – all-weather games area*

On the Rec

Benny pulled the lead

I held on tight

Daddy came with me

Daddy held on too.

Benny boy stopped

Sit said Dad

Benny boy sat

He stopped pulling the lead.

Benny can be a good dog!

Aimee Rickett

Why won't you look after me?

I'm choking!

Do you want me to fade away?

My heart is fading

Soon it will stop beating

Why can't you be green?

Why don't you love me?

I'm dirty. No, filthy!

Why build houses on me?

Listen to me! Why won't you?

I want to hear birds sing and see rabbits hop

Why won't you look after me?

I'm choking with gas.

Lydia Willmott

I am the oldest resident here in Fulbourn
It's changed a lot in my lifetime
No longer do gas-guzzling cars roam the streets endlessly
Instead there are electric cars whizzing around like little green bugs
The fields and the crops are as fresh as a daisy
And I finally managed to persuade the Council to expand the nature reserve
Of course, one man alone can't do all this
The community have made a tremendous effort
They created countless petitions
Some of them failed, most succeeded
That's how we got our wind farm
That's why there's no litter on the streets
And how we got the post office back
We refurbished the windmill instead of knocking it down
That's how we created a perfect village
Well, almost perfect.
We all make mistakes, and I'm no exception
I never should have approved the new factory
Or that cinema, still not complete after six months work
But there are only a few imperfections in our beautiful village
(We have to leave something for the next generation to do!)
Today's Fulbourn is more than just a village
It is a gift, my gift, in pristine condition
For the next generation.

Luke Wood

Deforestation Rap

Cutting down the trees is surely the worst, seeming as the earth needs them to breath. This is why the pandas are in danger cause .. we're .. cutting .. down the trees. CO2 and oxygen helps us and them too. We love the trees but they don't any moreas we come back with more and more chainsaws and 1 .. 2 .. 3 .. 4 we love the trees but they don't any more as we come back with more and more chainsaws.

1 2 3 4

We will protest for the last tree, it will stand strong, can't get us wrong, the machines are stripping us, breaking us, chopping us down, down, down, down, down. 1 2 3 4 let rain wash away all the pain from yesterday Hear the chainsaws once again 1 2 3 4 let the rain wash away all the pain from yesterday. Hear the chainsaws once again, this poem makes us feel strong no one can get us wrong by JayZ and Dexter Last

Jay Bayliss-Halsall and Declan Last

I, the village, give you food so you can eat
I give you water so you can drink
I give you a school so you can learn
I give you wide open spaces so you can run and play
I give you houses so you can live safely and well
I give you a community of friends so you can laugh and be loved
I give you beautifully scented flowers so you can enjoy the smells
I give you exciting wildlife so you can watch and wonder
I give you dark, soothing nights so you can rest and sleep
I give you early, bright mornings so you may wake alert, ready for your day
I give you roads and paths so you may travel and see the wonders of the world
I give you a community hall so you can socialise and bond
I give you a church so you can pray to our Almighty Lord
I give you parks so you can enjoy the summer breeze or the chill of snowball fights
I give you this poem to read and enjoy
Isn't it time you gave something back?

Lucy Crane

The village I see is full of rubbish on the streets
And we never hear the birds sing
Pollution pervades the air
The forest is gone!

The night is ferocious and nobody is safe
The shops are abandoned, empty like a desert
The village is buzzing incessantly like an angry wasp
And the fumes from the factories make me feel dizzy.

The rec is an industrial estate
I miss the children's games and laughter
Nobody ever goes to church – it stands empty and alone
There is hardly a blade of green grass to be seen.

I wish I hadn't agreed to build a factory
I wish I hadn't been so lazy in the protests
I should have been heard
I should have made a difference.

Sasha Arzumanova

Once I had a busy street, but now I'm empty – no-one walks there anymore

I used to be clean and welcoming, but now I'm dirty and grimy.

I used to feel sweet raindrops trickle down my throat

But the drops are now filled with smoke which ruins my life

I used to bear nutritious crops, but now they are dead

I used to be decorated with pretty houses but my people left me

They are gone

Trees grew and flowers bloomed before they were trashed.

I used to have a clean river until it became polluted

I used to have all those things until it turned into a disaster

I was murdered by the rubbish you fed me!

We are sorry we didn't care for you

We no longer cry for us, we cry for you and our mistakes

We wish we never took you out of existence

Callum Fordham

I want the river to be as clear as the blue sky as it trickles away with sparkling clouds
I want the villagers to be free like a swift swooping across the sky
I want the heart to be restored and the shops to be buzzing with life again
I want the rec to be greener and filled with laughing, tumbling children
I want more people to move in, just a few, and experience the love, the joy and the happiness
My perfect village

Maruth Alcantara

I've lived in Fulbourn for all of my 75 years and
Every one of those years I've loved watching the seasons
Through the trees.
I'm glad I donated money to preserve the
Windmill – a giant waving its hands over the village.
'Keep looking after our village,' I told the pupils at
Fulbourn Primary School.
I'm so glad I helped to plant more trees
In the nature reserve.
I remember when we demanded that the
Post office was re-opened.
When we all stopped the juggernauts
Charging through the village.
With trees in the woods the children can play.
When I look out of the window
I see families with children
Running beneath the branches.
Fulbourn is green.
With the post office re-opened Fulbourn is feeling like it used to.
I'm so proud we made Fulbourn a better place for the children!
But look out, youngsters!
The juggernauts could come back so
Look after our village!

Connor Childerley

Lightning Source UK Ltd.
Milton Keynes UK

173968UK00001B/5/P

9 781845 494940